Sweet Indulgences

Sweet Indulgences

DESSERTS FOR EVERY OCCASION

Norman Kolpas

FRIEDMAN/FAIRFAX PUBLISHERS

ISBN 1-56799-022-3

Editor: Stephen Williams
Designer: Judy Morgan
Photography Editor: Ede Rothaus

Typeset by The Interface Group, Inc.
Color separations by Scantrans Ltd.
Printed and bound in Hong Kong by Leefung-Asco Printers Ltd.

For bulk purchases and special sales, please contact:
Friedman/Fairfax Publishers
15 West 26th Street
New York, NY 10010
(212) 685-6610 FAX (212) 685-1307

Acknowledgements

Michael Friedman and Karla Olson deserve thanks for suggesting that I tackle the subject of entertaining with desserts, and Stephen Williams, as always, has shown remarkable tact and grace in his editing. Thanks are also due to their colleagues at Tern Enterprise in New York, and the staff at Price Stern Sloan in Los Angeles, for all the efforts taken on behalf of this book.

Once again, my wife, Katie, has earned abundant thanks. She's the one who endures all the testing and the writing, and yet remains capable of cheerfully asking the question, "What's for dessert?"

Contents

"What's for dessert?"
That may be the most-asked question at dinner tables worldwide. Nothing in the realm of food captures our imaginations more powerfully than the final course of a meal. This book offers dozens of answers to that question, with a comprehensive selection of cold and hot, familiar and exotic, simple and elaborate desserts.

In the first half of Sweet Indulgences, you'll find a variety of recipes grouped according to their main ingredients. Want something nutty? Turn to the "Nuts and Dried Fruits" section on page 50. Craving a chocolate indulgence? Look no further than page 56. How about a fresh fruit dessert? See page 46. In addition to several recipes, each section gives useful, basic information on the ingredients in question, to help you create original desserts.

But Sweet Indulgences is more than just a recipe book. In these pages you'll find imaginative new solutions to a problem frequently encountered by everyone who loves to share good food with friends and family—finding a new way to entertain.

Here are seven different menus for fabulous dessert parties like Chocoholic Heaven (page 118), with a menu of Double Chocolate Irish Cream Fudge Cake,

Individual Mexican Chocolate Mousses, Mandarin Chocolate Sherbet and other chocolate temptations, and the comparatively guilt-free Light Summer Indulgences party (page 86) which lets you off the hook with Seasonal Berry Salad, Tropical Sorbet Medley, Light Cookies and more.

Let your guests create their own fantastic desserts at the Create-a-Crêpe Party, (page 76) which details how to make wonderfully light crepes that guests can fill with a variety of toppings, including Berries Jubilee, Wet Walnut Sauce and Suzette Topping. Or for a more casual party, invite friends over for an Ice Cream and Frozen Yogurt Sundae Bar (page 106), where they can concoct sundaes made with Extra-Rocky Road Ice Cream, Cappucino Frozen Yogurt, Bittersweet Chocolate Sauce and Old-Fashioned Marshmallow Sauce.

Each menu includes helpful guidelines for decorating your home and getting as much of the work as possible done in advance so you can enjoy the evening along with your guests.

All that's left for you to do is something that's never too hard when desserts are involved: Indulge yourself.

Entertaining with Desserts

No course of the meal is more eagerly anticipated than dessert. And because it is the last course you serve, dessert gives you the best chance to give guests a favorable memory of the meal to take home.

That's not to say that dessert has to be a spectacle that calls for a culinary Cecil B. DeMille. Rather, the appropriateness of the dessert you serve, and the way in which you offer it to your guests, is what matters.

The following strategies will help you choose what kind of dessert to make and decide how to serve it.

The Selection

Never forget that unless you are having a party centered exclusively around sweets, your dessert buffet is part of the entire meal. The first factor to consider when choosing what dessert to serve is what kinds of dishes will precede it.

Pay attention to the flavors, textures and richness of the other dishes in the meal. Then plan your dessert accordingly. Was the main course heavy and rich? Then maybe it's best to let your guests' tastebuds unwind with a light fruit dessert. Were the flavors of the meal hot and spicy? Perhaps something creamy and cooling is called for to conclude things. Was the entire dinner prior to dessert light and saintly calorie-wise? Then you're justified in splurging on a truly indulgent dessert.

Then again, maybe you want to continue in the lighter vein. That kind of decision will depend as much on your own tastes as on the tastes and needs of the other people sharing your food. Give some thought to the dietary needs and interests of your guests; if you have any doubt, ask them in advance. It's not a good experience when you serve a dessert and find that one or more of your guests can't eat it. Better to come up with an alternative that everyone can enjoy, or to compromise by offering two different desserts from which guests can choose.

The season is another factor in your choice of desserts, affecting that last course as it does all the others. Winter's cold calls for hearty, comforting desserts—hot cobblers and crumbles, rich puddings—but the heat of summer makes us yearn for light sweets that cool and refresh us.

Finally, the style of the occasion will influence your dessert choice. An elegant dinner party calls for simple, sophisticated desserts—long-stemmed glasses of sorbet, plates of elegant cookies or premium chocolate truffles. A humble, family-style supper invites the kinds of desserts —satisfying custards, heaping sundaes, rich cheesecakes— that you really want to tuck into.

The Dessert Party

Sometimes dessert can be an event in its own right. Having friends over for a party of sweets is a truly delightful way to entertain.

A dessert party allows you to go all out and yet expend less effort than you would if you were serving a dinner party of three courses or more. It also gives you a time limit —the hours after dinner or, occasionally, the hours between lunch and dinner.

The occasions for hosting a dessert party can be as varied as for any other type of party: a birthday; an anniversary; a graduation; a special visit from out-of-town friends or relatives; the change of the seasons; a festive holiday; or simply a get-together with friends. You can invite just a few people or a crowd. And it can be as casual or as formal as you like, from blue jeans to black tie.

Plan your menu to match the occasion and the number of people you've invited. Two or three desserts is a sufficient amount for a small gathering, while a dessert buffet of five or more specialties may be in order for a larger party. If people are elegantly dressed, serve them stylish, easy-to-eat desserts that aren't likely to drip or splash on their best party clothes—individual dishes of mousse or sorbet, bite-size dipped chocolates, and so on. Let guests at a casual gathering enjoy messy-but-fun, do-it-yourself kinds of desserts— sundae bars, chocolate fondues and the like.

Make variety the spice of your dessert table: Offer different kinds of desserts featuring several main ingredients. Include desserts that both complement and contrast with each other—something based on chocolate and something with fresh fruit; crisp cookies and soft, creamy flans; bite-size candies and slice-it-yourself cheesecakes or tortes. Or let the exception prove the rule, and offer an extravaganza of desserts that share a common theme—the best fruits of the season, for example, or that near-universal object of passion, chocolate.

In the second half of this book, you'll find menus for special dessert parties. Use them as models for your own party, or as starting points for your own imagination.

The Guest List

As much as the desserts themselves, your guests play a large part in the success or failure of your dessert party.

It may seem obvious to say, but it's important to pay attention to your guest list, inviting a compatible mix of people who will strike the kind of social sparks that make a party take off. Imagine which guests might enjoy each other's company. If one of the guests is shy, or has some special interest, try to invite someone who might draw him or her out. And be sure to bear special tastes or needs in mind as you plan your menu.

© Greg Kopacka/Stock Imagery

The Strategy

A little advance planning for your dessert party will go a long way toward ensuring that the event is a dazzling success.

Before you do anything, make sure you're absolutely familiar with the recipes you plan to prepare and serve. Read the recipes thoroughly and draw up a complete shopping list of ingredients and any special utensils you might need. Then check the list over, noting those shops you frequent that might carry specific items. Then reorganize the list by store, so you'll shop quickly and with as few stops as possible.

Draw up a time line—as rough or neat as you like—to show how far in advance you can complete various stages of the recipes. You might want to list the recipes down the left-hand side of the chart, and the advance preparation scheduling (for example, A Week Before, Two Days Ahead, Night Before, Morning Before, Three Hours Before, One Hour Before, Last Minute) along the top. Then chart each recipe's preparation on this grid and tack up the chart in a prominent place in your kitchen. You might get added satisfaction from marking off each stage with a pen as you complete it.

Save some room on the chart, or make a separate one, for any non-food-related preparations: picking up rental glasses, punch bowls or coffee urns for a large gathering; setting the table; picking up flowers; retrieving the tablecloth from the cleaner's; setting the table; visiting the record store for the latest sounds; and so on.

Setting the Dessert Buffet Table

It used to be that at home desserts were most often displayed on a sideboard buffet. And many restaurants today show pride in their desserts by setting them out on a sideboard or special dessert cart.

For your own dessert buffet, the best possible setting—one that best shows off the desserts and allows guests the room to serve themselves without crowding—is the dining room table. Depending on the size and style of the gathering, though, you could also arrange the desserts on the kitchen counter, or on the coffee table, or at various places around the house—encouraging guests to wander and mingle as they search out new sweet treats. If you like, you can even go for an old-fashioned effect, pushing the dining table up against the wall, turning it into a commodious sideboard.

For presenting your desserts, you'll need several large serving dishes or platters. Even desserts that come in individual glasses or dishes can look extra special if the small servings are placed on a large, attractive tray. For hot-from-the-oven desserts, you'll need to set out iron or ceramic trivets or heat-proof pads to protect your serving table. Although certain hot desserts are just as delicious when they cool down, others—such as hot ice cream sauces, chocolate fondues and baked puddings—stay at their best with the aid of an electrically heated serving tray or a chafing dish heated by a small flame before the party (be sure to check that you have enough of the right fuel for the heating element and that it's working properly).

Desserts that are best chilled—from fresh fruit to homemade ice cream—can be presented on beds of crushed ice. Set your container of ice cream inside a large container—a bowl or an ice bucket, for example—filled with the ice. Place fresh fruits on a platter set atop a layer of ice held by a larger platter that has a rim to hold the water as the ice melts.

Set out at least two individual serving plates or bowls per person, so that your guests can enjoy several different desserts without incompatible flavors mingling or causing an unappetizing mess. Include an equal number of small dessert forks and spoons—whatever's appropriate to the dishes you're serving. And be prepared for the possibility that you may have to wash up some plates and utensils quickly during the party to ensure a fresh supply. And have plenty of folded napkins on hand. Small cocktail napkins will do and, unless you're throwing a truly elegant party that demands your best linens, don't shy away from using good quality paper napkins.

Steven Mark Needham/Envision

Coffee, Tea and After-Dinner Drinks

Most of your guests will also welcome a glass of something to accompany their desserts. Coffee is the common denominator and, in this day and age, it's a good idea to offer decaffeinated as well as regular coffee—particularly since your dessert party is most likely to be an evening occasion.

Brew up fresh coffee—preferably from freshly ground beans—and keep a constant supply coming. It's worth investing in one of the attractive vacuum thermos pitchers now available to keep the coffee hot on the serving table; hot plates tend to give coffee an unpleasant, muddy flavor, and if you're a conscientious host you'll only find yourself throwing out each potful before it has all been poured. Be sure to label clearly which pitcher is decaffeinated and which is regular to avoid any unpleasant surprises for your guests. Have plenty of coffee cups and saucers—or, if it's an informal occasion, mugs—set out on the table, along with small pitchers of milk and half-and-half, a bowl of sugar, another containing packets of sugar substitute and spoons for stirring.

Among the most pleasurable beverages of all to enjoy with dessert are those based on espresso. Traditionally, espresso is made by forcing pressurized, steaming-hot water through very finely ground, extra-dark-roasted coffee; the result is a powerful, inky-black brew that many connoisseurs consider the very essence of coffee. Until fairly recently, the best espresso machines were large, very costly models. In the past few years, though, a number of manufacturers have brought out kitchen countertop models that are reasonably priced.

Serve espresso in small, demitasse cups. Offer a strip of fresh lemon zest or peel with each serving for guests to rub around the rims of their cups or twist and drop into the espresso. If you like, put the espresso in a larger cup and add frothy steamed milk—just a good splash and a few spoonfuls of foam for a traditional *cappucino*, or an equal amount or more of milk for a *caffe latte*. Some people like to dust the foam with a little cocoa powder or ground cinnamon. For a decadent variation, you can add a shot of after-dinner brandy or liqueur to your milky espresso drink. Cognac or any chocolate, orange or other sweet fruit-flavored liqueurs are excellent choices. If you want to go really overboard, replace the steamed milk with a generous dollop of freshly whipped cream, spooned into the cup just before serving.

For guests who prefer tea, offer a selection of good quality bagged varieties—including several different tea blends, along with caffeine-free herbal blends. Keep a kettle of water simmering on the kitchen stove.

Depending on the occasion, some of your guests may also welcome something stronger with their desserts. Have a separate serving tray with a good bottle of brandy or cognac; a selection of your favorite liqueurs, including such classic fruit flavors as orange (Grand Marnier), raspberry (framboise), and cherry (kirsch); any other liqueurs that strike your fancy; and small brandy snifters and liqueur glasses.

Setting a Style

The dessert menus that follow include suggestions for setting a particular mood with tableware. But you don't have to run out and spend hundreds of dollars on new dishes, platters and cutlery.

You can create a special mood for your dessert party in a number of other simple ways. Just one special piece of tableware—whether it's a cherished wedding present, a family heirloom or something you picked up for next to nothing at the local thrift shop—can enhance the mood. Add other decorative elements to the table to heighten the atmosphere: interesting fabric table coverings; various candles and candlesticks; fresh seasonal flowers; and a selection of your favorite collectibles arranged as a novel centerpiece. Your only limit in setting a unique table is your imagination.

Music, too, can enhance the mood. Let the occasion and the style of desserts you're serving determine what you play. But don't let the music dominate the party; the main sound you should hear as the party progresses is the conversation and laughter of your guests.

The Party in Progress

With all the advance preparation and planning done, your dessert party should run like clockwork. Go through one final check on your preparations an hour or so before guests arrive to make sure that the desserts are at whatever stage they should be and the table is completely set and ready. If any desserts are meant to be served fresh from the oven, preheat them. Remove desserts from the freezer that need to soften at room temperature before they're served. Be ready to reheat any warm sauces that you may have prepared in advance and refrigerated.

Be sure the coffee and drinks are ready to serve the moment the guests start arriving and that the desserts are on display, ready to be enjoyed. Let the oven timer tell you when hot dishes should come out and you'll be free to enjoy the beginning of your party.

As more guests arrive, keep an eye out for any dishes that may need replenishing or any individual serving plates that guests may be finished with. Aside from the occasional trip you make to the kitchen to get more food and bus a few dishes, the party should pretty much run itself.

A Word on Help

Fairly small dessert gatherings can be run smoothly by one or two people. However, don't play the brave soldier and go it alone if you're mounting a large gathering. Your telephone directory should have listings for maids, butlers, party planners, bartenders and other people who can help your party run more smoothly, from setup to the last dirty dish.

Your friends may be able to recommend reliable people who've helped them, and you can get referrals for student workers from the local high school, college or university. Hiring help may cost a little, but it's a small price to pay for the privilege of enjoying your own party.

Cleanup

The party may be over. But before you can call it a day, you'll have to clean up (unless, of course, you hired some help).

Fortunately, that cleanup should be pretty easy. With all the advance preparation you'll have done, the basic cookware will have long since been washed and tidied away. What's left? Just the serving dishes and utensils, individual plates and bowls, forks and spoons, cups, mugs and any liqueur glasses or brandy snifters.

You'll have done a good bit of the clearing while the party was underway, stacking used dishes and piling cutlery neatly near the kitchen sink; the remainder can be cleared at the very end of the party. Cleanup can then proceed along fairly methodical lines. Your first and most important task is to remove food from the plates and pack away and store any leftover desserts before they have a chance to spoil.

That done, you may want to enjoy that last cup of coffee or a final snifter of brandy with your spouse or a few lingering friends before you face another dish. And who says you can't just leave the dishes until the morning, to be washed after you've enjoyed a good night's sleep and put the cap on a wonderful evening of entertaining?

Dessert Basics

Far too many people perceive dessert making as an arcane art that calls for secret knowledge and magical skills to create something even remotely edible—let alone delicious and beautiful.

That's not the case. True, there are special techniques you'll use when making desserts that you won't need when you prepare the rest of the meal. And some desserts do call for more elaborate preparation in many more stages than you're likely to encounter in recipes for most savory dishes.

But, as with most specialized knowledge, if you start with the basics and work your way up from there, soon you'll find that you've unwittingly become an expert. And the key to expertise in dessert making lies in the basic ingredients. Learn to whisk an egg white, toast a tray of nuts, caramelize sugar, melt chocolate over a double boiler or any of the other basic ingredient-related tasks, and you're well on the way to being a master of desserts.

That's why the following section is organized by the fundamental ingredients of desserts. One by one, it introduces them to you and offers basic, delicious recipes that embody the techniques you'll use to make all types of sweet indulgences.

Introductory notes to the recipes explain the techniques, offering the simple tips and hints you'll need to produce successful results. Many of the recipes also include suggestions for varying the ingredients. Feel free to use them as a starting point from which to create original desserts.

23

© Gordon E. Smith

MILK AND CREAM

Milk and cream seem to be the very essences of dessert—they're both pure, rich and satisfying. Both ingredients, of course, appear in many dessert recipes—in custards, cakes, crêpes, puddings and so on.

Milk and cream can be transformed into wonderful ingredients, such as the whipped cream that garnishes so many desserts. Because the butterfat in cream traps air when it's beaten with a whisk, the richer the cream you use, the better it whips up. And unlike egg whites, which trap air better at room temperature, cream whips up best when it is chilled. The reason is simple: Cold solidifies the fat in the cream, making it thicker.

And in one particular dessert, milk and cream reign supreme: ice cream. It's no surprise that ice cream is such a popular dessert. There's something simple, yet so delicious, about it—whether sinfully enriched with egg yolks and heavy cream or made lighter with fewer eggs and milk instead of cream. Ice cream has even become a light dessert of late—in the guise of frozen yogurt.

But ice cream isn't something to ponder seriously for too long. As the playwright Thornton Wilder so neatly summed it up, "My advice to you is not to inquire why or whither, but just enjoy your ice-cream while it's on your plate—that's my philosophy."

Vanilla Bean White Chocolate Chip Ice Cream

This is the ultimate vanilla ice cream, with the added surprise of rich chunks of white chocolate which, camouflaged by their color, won't be noticed until you and your guests bite into them. Most good-size supermarkets or gourmet stores carry high-quality white chocolate.

If you like soft ice cream, this can be served the moment it's done churning. Or you can make it several hours ahead and let it harden in the freezer. The ice cream will stay in peak serving condition for up to a week.

For an extra-lavish presentation, pour a shot of your favorite fruit liqueur over a dish of the ice cream.

1 quart heavy cream

1 vanilla bean, split in half lengthwise

4 egg yolks

1 cup sugar

1/2 pound white chocolate, coarsely chopped

In a heavy saucepan over medium heat, warm the cream just until bubbles appear around the edge of the pan. Add the vanilla bean, cover the pan, remove it from the heat and let the cream steep for about 15 minutes.

Meanwhile, in a mixing bowl, beat together the egg yolks and sugar with a wire whisk until the mixture is thick and pale yellow, 3 to 5 minutes.

Remove the vanilla bean from the cream. With the tip of a small, sharp knife, scrape the vanilla seeds from the inside of the bean into the cream, discarding the shell. Then, whisking continuously, gradually pour the cream into the yolk mixture.

Return the mixture to the saucepan and stir over very low heat just until it is thick enough to coat a spoon, 3 to 5 minutes. Remove from the heat and set the bottom of the pan inside a baking pan filled with ice and water. Continue stirring the mixture until it cools to room temperature.

Freeze the mixture in an ice-cream maker, following manufacturer's directions. When it is thick but still soft enough to stir, add the chopped white chocolate. Serve immediately, or transfer to the freezer to harden.

Makes 1/2 gallon

© Jeffry W. Myers/FPG International

Peach Melba Frozen Yogurt

The classic dessert combination of fresh peaches and raspberry sauce over vanilla ice cream finds a light new life in this easy-to-make dessert.

You can, of course, make an infinite number of variations of it—substituting apricots or nectarines for the peaches; strawberries, blueberries or boysenberries for the raspberries; making a raspberry yogurt with a peach swirl; or combining any other soft, juicy fruits that strike your fancy. And by all means use defrosted frozen fruit, or even canned fruit drained of its syrup, if fresh isn't available.

If you want to make an extra-rich dessert, use whole-milk yogurt. Conversely, you can lower the calorie count by substituting nonfat yogurt for the lowfat.

If you like soft frozen yogurt, this can be served up the moment it's done churning. Or you can make it several hours ahead and let it harden in the freezer. The yogurt will stay in peak serving condition for up to a week.

1 cup packed fresh, skinned and sliced peaches

1¹/₃ cups sugar

1 quart plain lowfat yogurt

1/2 teaspoon vanilla extract

1 cup fresh raspberries

In a food processor or blender, puree the peaches with 1 cup of the sugar.

Put the peaches, yogurt and vanilla in an ice-cream maker and start to freeze them, following manufacturer's instructions.

As soon as you start the machine, puree the raspberries with the remaining sugar in the processor or blender. Then press the puree through a fine sieve to remove the seeds.

Transfer the raspberry puree to a small saucepan and simmer over medium to low heat, stirring constantly, until it is thick and syrupy, 5 to 7 minutes. Set the bottom of the pan in a bowl or pan of ice and water and stir to cool the syrup to room temperature.

When the yogurt mixture is frozen thick but still soft, remove it from the machine and, with a rubber spatula, fold in the raspberry syrup, swirling it through the mixture. Serve immediately, or transfer the yogurt to the freezer to harden.

Makes 1/2 gallon

BUTTER

It seems almost too obvious to say that butter is an essential ingredient in dessert making. Where would cakes, cookies and pastries be without the richness of butter?

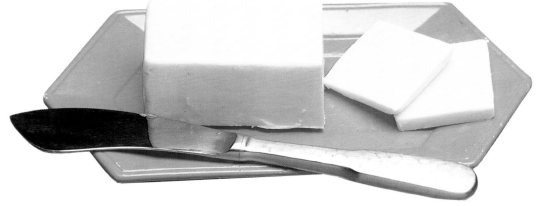

Of course you can substitute other shortenings for butter; we've all eaten commercial baked goods prepared with margarine or vegetable shortening. But, on first bite of those ersatz treats, butter's virtue becomes clear by its absence: Nothing can compare to the taste of good, pure dairy butter.

And in that respect, butter doesn't just help certain desserts—it *defines* them. What would you call a classic buttercream pastry filling if you made it without butter? Could you serve a "butter cookie" made with margarine?

When you choose butter for desserts, be sure to opt for unsalted, or sweet, butter; the salt in ordinary butter makes it a tad too savory for after-dinner consumption. Store your butter in a covered butter dish in the refrigerator, away from foods whose odors it might absorb. If you buy it one pound (four sticks) at a time, store the extras in the freezer, where they'll keep well; but be sure to let the rock-hard frozen butter come back to refrigerator or room temperature before use.

Chocolate Rum Butter Sandwiches

Two classic buttery dessert preparations—
a buttercream filling and crisp butter
cookies—are paired in these sandwich
cookies. They'll keep fresh for several days
if you store them in an airtight container
in a cool place.

Chocolate Cookies

1/2 pound unsalted butter, at room
temperature

1/2 cup sugar

1 egg yolk

Pinch of salt

1 teaspoon vanilla extract

10 tablespoons cocoa powder

1³/4 cups all-purpose flour

Rum Buttercream

2/3 cup sugar

1/2 cup warm water

5 egg yolks, at room temperature

1/2 pound unsalted butter, at room
temperature, cut into tablespoon-size chunks

1¹/2 tablespoons dark rum

For the cookies, cream together the butter
and sugar in a food processor or electric
mixer. Add the egg yolk, salt and vanilla
and continue processing or mixing until
thoroughly blended; then blend in the
cocoa powder.

Add the flour and pulse the machine or
mix just until it is incorporated. Put the
processor or mixing bowl in the refrigerator to chill for about 15 minutes.

On a lightly floured work surface, divide
the dough into 3 equal pieces and roll it
into logs 2 inches in diameter. Roll each
log in waxed paper and refrigerate for at
least 1 hour.

Preheat the oven to 350°F.

With a small, sharp knife, cut each log
into 1/8-inch-thick slices, placing the slices
on a cookie sheet lined with parchment
paper. Bake until the cookies just begin to
brown at the edges, about 10 minutes.
Transfer to a wire rack to cool.

While the cookies are cooling, prepare
the buttercream. First, put the sugar and
water in a heavy saucepan and let them
stand for about 10 minutes; then, over low
heat, stir just until the sugar dissolves.
Raise the heat to medium and bring the
syrup to a boil; boil briefly, no more than
about 20 seconds, just until the syrup
forms a thin thread when dripped from a
spoon dipped into the pan, or measures
about 215°F on a candy thermometer.
Remove the syrup from the heat.

Put the egg yolks in mixing bowl and
whisk until smooth. Then, whisking continuously, slowly pour the syrup into the
yolks; continue whisking until the mixture is cool, light and fluffy.

A few pieces at a time, whisk the butter
into the egg yolk mixture until thoroughly
incorporated, to form a rich, thick cream.
Then whisk in the rum.

To assemble the cookies, spoon the buttercream into a pastry bag fitted with a
wide piping tip. Pick up a cookie and pipe
about a 1/8-inch layer of filling, just over 2
teaspoons, onto its underside; then gently
place the underside of another cookie up
against the filling to form a compact sandwich, pressing to spread the filling up to
the edge of the cookies. Continue with
the remaining cookies and filling.

Store the cookies in an airtight container in a cool place.

Makes 3 dozen sandwiches

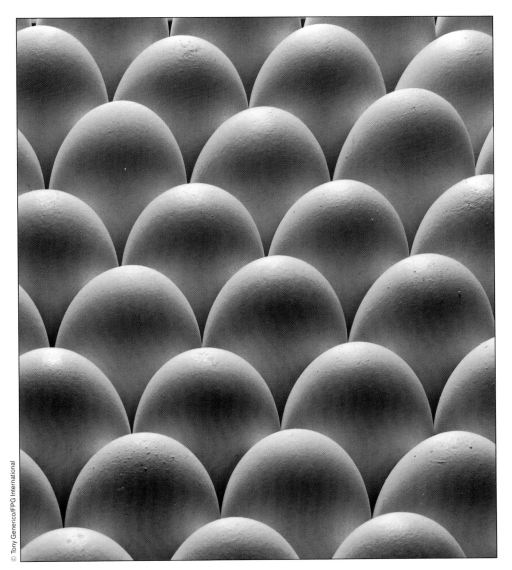

© Tony Generico/FPG International

EGGS

Nowhere in cuisine is the egg's versatility more apparent than in desserts.

Apart from the egg's many supporting roles—aerating and binding cakes, glazing piecrusts, enriching ice creams —there are a number of recipes in which it stars, most notably custards, soufflés and meringues.

The egg recipes that follow call for medium to large eggs that weigh from one and three-quarters to two and one-quarter ounces each. If your eggs are slightly larger or smaller, you may want to adjust proportions accordingly.

Though eggs will keep well at cool room temperature or in the refrigerator for several weeks, aim to use the freshest you can buy. To test an egg for freshness, simply place it, in the shell, in a bowl filled with warm water; a fresh egg will sink to the bottom; a stale one will float. For the best results in dessert recipes, let the eggs come to room temperature before using them.

Be sure to store eggs away from strong-smelling foods. Their shells are porous and could absorb odors you might not want to have in your favorite dessert.

Custards—A classic custard is a gentle marriage of eggs and milk, cooked slowly—with the aid of a double boiler or hot-water bath to mitigate the heat—until thick and rich.

It seems as if every nation has its variation on the baked custard, from the classic French crème caramel to the Mexican Cinnamon-Coffee Flan and the Caribbean-influenced Coconut Custard that follow. Stirred custard reaches its pinnacle in Crème Brulée—a thick custard cream topped with burnt sugar—which many enterprising cooks enrich by adding fresh seasonal fruits.

© Steven Mark Needham/Envision

Mexican Cinnamon-Coffee Flan

This variation on a classic crème caramel adds the favorite Mexican flavorings of cinnamon, coffee and vanilla. Make the individual flans the day before, and keep them covered with plastic wrap in the refrigerator.

Cinnamon Caramel

1 cup sugar

1/2 cup water

1 teaspoon ground cinnamon

Coffee Custard

1 cup whipping cream

1 cup milk

2 heaping teaspoons instant coffee granules

1/2 teaspoon vanilla extract

3 eggs

2 egg yolks

1/2 cup brown sugar

Pinch of salt

For the cinnamon caramel, put the sugar, water and cinnamon into a small saucepan and bring to a boil over medium heat, stirring constantly until the sugar dissolves. Continue boiling, without stirring, until the syrup turns a medium golden brown, 5 to 7 minutes. Immediately remove it from the heat and divide it equally among 6 individual custard cups, turning each cup to evenly coat its bottom and sides.

For the custard, put the cream and milk in a medium saucepan over medium heat. As soon as the liquid is hot and begins to form bubbles at the side of the pan, remove it from the heat and stir in the coffee and vanilla.

Meanwhile, in a mixing bowl, lightly beat together the eggs, egg yolks, sugar and salt with a small whisk.

Preheat the oven to 325°F. Bring a kettle of water to a boil.

Stirring continuously with the whisk, slowly pour 6 ounces of the milk mixture into the egg mixture. Pour this back into the remaining milk and stir to blend. Pour the mixture through a fine sieve.

Distribute the flan mixture evenly among the caramel-coated cups, and put the cups in a shallow baking pan. Open the oven, pull out a shelf and place the pan on it; then carefully pour boiling water into the baking pan to come halfway up the sides of the custard cups, and carefully slide the shelf into the oven.

Bake until a small, sharp knife inserted into the center of a flan comes out clean, 20 to 25 minutes. Let the custards cool to room temperature, then refrigerate.

Before serving, run a small, sharp knife around the edge of each flan to loosen it from its cup. Place an upside-down individual serving plate over a cup and, holding them tightly together, swiftly turn them over, shaking downward slightly to dislodge the flan. Carefully lift off the cup before serving.

Makes 6 servings

© Michael A. Keller/FPG International

Coconut Custard

This classic baked egg dessert is given a Caribbean twist with the addition of coconut. Make the custard up to one day ahead, keeping it covered with plastic wrap in the refrigerator. To further emphasize the tropical note, accompany the custard with fresh mango or papaya slices. You'll need to have cheesecloth on hand to make this recipe.

3 cups milk

1/2 cup plus 2 tablespoons shredded coconut

2 eggs

1 egg yolk

2 tablespoons sugar

Pinch of salt

2 tablespoons unsalted butter, at room temperature

Put the milk and ¹/₂ cup of coconut in a medium saucepan. Bring to a boil over medium heat, reduce the heat and simmer until the milk has reduced to 2 cups, about 20 minutes.

Meanwhile, in a mixing bowl, lightly beat together the eggs, egg yolk, sugar and salt with a small whisk.

Preheat the oven to 325°F. Bring a kettle of water to a boil.

Pour the milk through a strainer lined with cheesecloth; discard the coconut. Stirring continuously with the whisk, slowly pour 6 ounces of the hot milk into the egg mixture. Pour this mixture into the remaining milk and stir to blend.

Generously rub the insides of 6 individual custard cups with the butter. Distribute the custard mixture evenly among them, and put the cups in a shallow baking pan. Open the oven, pull out a shelf and carefully place the pan on it; then pour boiling water into the baking pan to come halfway up the sides of the custard cups, and slide the shelf into the oven.

Bake until a small, sharp knife inserted into the center of a custard cup comes out clean, about 20 minutes. Let the custard cool to room temperature, then refrigerate.

Before serving, preheat the oven to 350°F. Spread the remaining shredded coconut on a sheet of aluminum foil, and toast it in the oven until golden brown, about 15 minutes. Let it cool a few minutes, and sprinkle it over the individual cups of custard. Serve directly from the cups.

Makes 6 servings

Crème Brulée with Fresh Summer Fruit

You will need a double boiler for this recipe. Use whatever summer fruits are at their best and juiciest—berries, peaches and nectarines are my favorite choices. You can prepare the custard up to a day ahead. Assemble the final individual crème brulées just moments before you serve them.

2 cups whipping cream

6 egg yolks

1/4 cup sugar

1 teaspoon cornstarch

1 teaspoon vanilla extract

3/4 cup fresh summer fruit (skinned and sliced peaches or nectarines; sliced strawberries; whole raspberries, boysenberries or blueberries)

9 tablespoons light brown sugar

In the top of a double boiler, heat the cream just until bubbles begin to form at the side. Remove from the heat.

In a mixing bowl, beat the eggs with a wire whisk until smooth and light yellow in color. Toss together the sugar and cornstarch and gradually beat them in. Then, whisking continuously, slowly pour in the hot cream.

Return the mixture to the top of the double boiler, and cook over a gentle simmer, stirring constantly, until the custard is thick enough to coat a spoon, 15 to 20 minutes. Remove from the heat and stir in the vanilla. Pour through a fine sieve, then let the custard cool to room temperature, stirring occasionally.

Distribute the fruit evenly on the bottoms of 6 individual custard cups or 1/2-cup soufflé molds. Pour the custard over it, smoothing the surface evenly, leaving a 1/8-inch space between the custard and the rim of the cup. Cover with plastic wrap and refrigerate.

Before serving, preheat the broiler. Put the cups in a baking pan filled with cold water and ice to come halfway up the sides of the cups. Evenly sprinkle the brown sugar over the custards to cover them completely.

Place the pan under the broiler and, keeping a close eye on the custards, broil just until the sugar is completely melted and bubbly, 2 to 3 minutes. Remove immediately and serve.

Makes 6 servings

© Burke/Triolo

Soufflés—Light and ethereal, yet rich and satisfying, the soufflé is considered by many to be the ultimate dessert.

Such sublimity has led to the myth that soufflés are impossible to make, that mixing them is high science and that, once they're in the oven, you must tiptoe lest they fall. But soufflés aren't really that difficult, as long as you bear in mind that what makes them rise is, naturally enough, air.

Every step of a soufflé's preparation is aimed at incorporating as much air as possible into the finished product and keeping it there. Begin with the eggs at room temperature, since the whites will whip up fluffier.

Be sure to separate the eggs carefully; any speck of yolk in the whites will keep them from rising to their peak. To separate an egg, carefully crack it against the side of a bowl and then transfer the yolk back and forth between the shell halves, letting the white drop into the bowl below. Or, if you like using your hands, you can empty the egg onto your fingers and let the white drip down between them; the yolk will rest on top, provided it didn't break when you cracked the shell. Some cautious cooks break and separate each egg over a small bowl, making sure the separation is successful before transferring the yolk and white to separate, larger bowls.

Beat the whites with a wire whisk in a roomy hemispherical bowl; experts claim that an unlined copper bowl is best, since a reaction with the metal helps the whites hold air better; but it isn't absolutely essential (don't use aluminum, though; it discolors eggs). Whip the whites until they barely form stiff peaks when the whisk is lifted out—the optimal stage for a soufflé with a consistency that is at once tender and firm.

Once they've been beaten, use the egg whites immediately, or they will begin to deflate. Gently combined with the soufflé base—any sweet, egg-yolk-thickened mixture flavored with fresh fruit, liqueur or chocolate—the egg whites are quickly baked in soufflé dishes that have been coated with a mixture of sugar and butter that helps the airy mixture climb ever higher.

Bittersweet Chocolate-Almond Soufflé

Here is a soufflé mixture with a truly adult taste, derived from bittersweet chocolate and those little Italian dry macaroons known as *amaretti*. Have all your ingredients ready in advance—the eggs separated, the chocolate grated and so on. Then, at the end of the meal, excuse yourself from your guests—or invite them into the kitchen to keep you company—and whisk the egg whites before combining them with the other ingredients and baking the soufflés.

2 tablespoons unsalted butter, at room temperature

2 tablespoons granulated sugar

6 eggs, at room temperature

6 ounces bittersweet chocolate, finely grated

6 small Italian amaretti, finely crumbled

1/4 cup superfine sugar

1 cup heavy cream, lightly whipped

Preheat the oven to 350°F.

Butter the insides of 6 individual soufflé cups, and sprinkle them evenly with the granulated sugar.

Break the eggs and separate the whites from the yolks, taking care that no yolk gets into the whites. Put the yolks in a mixing bowl, and whisk them until thick and smooth. Whisk in the chocolate, amaretti and sugar until thoroughly combined, then set the mixture aside.

In a separate mixing bowl, with a clean whisk beat the egg whites until they form stiff peaks when the whisk is lifted out. With a rubber spatula, gently fold about a quarter of the whites into the egg yolk mixture; then pour that mixture into the bowl of egg whites, and gently fold with the spatula just until combined.

Immediately divide the soufflé mixture between the prepared cups. Place them in the oven and bake until well puffed, 8 to 10 minutes. Serve immediately with whipped cream for guests to spoon into the center of their soufflés.

Makes 6 servings

Meringues—Egg whites alone, beaten stiff, combined with sugar and then cooked, become the ever popular meringue. Airy and sweet, meringue is the ultimate answer to the dessert request for something light, and it's at its most definitive in the classic French dessert called *oeufs à la neige,* "snow eggs," floating on a base of light egg custard.

© Burke/Triolo

Snow Eggs with Anise Custard

The anise-flavored liqueur called Sambuca gives this new version of a classic dessert its own distinctive flavor.

You can prepare this dessert well in advance, poaching the meringue eggs and making the custard several hours ahead and refrigerating them, to be assembled just before serving. If you do, though, be sure to cover the custard's surface with plastic wrap to prevent a skin from forming; keep the meringue eggs in a single layer in a covered dish, to keep their shapes pristine and prevent them from drying. The dish is as good served right out of the refrigerator as it is warm and freshly made.

6 eggs, separated

2 cups confectioners' sugar

3 cups milk

3/4 cup sugar

1 vanilla bean, split in half lengthwise

1 1/2 tablespoons Sambuca liqueur

3 ounces bittersweet chocolate (optional), broken into pieces

In a large bowl, beat the egg whites until they form soft peaks. Continue whisking as you gradually add the confectioners' sugar, beating the whites until they form a meringue with stiff peaks. Set the whites aside.

Put the milk in a medium saucepan with half the granulated sugar and the vanilla bean. Over medium heat, bring it to a gentle boil; reduce the heat to a bare simmer. With a large dessert spoon, scoop up a heaping spoonful of the meringue; round the top of the spoonful with another spoon to make an egg shape, then ease it into the simmering milk. Repeat with several more spoonfuls, taking care not to overcrowd the pan. Poach the meringue eggs until firm, 2 to 3 minutes per side, turning them gently with a spoon; then transfer them to a large, shallow serving platter with a raised rim or to individual shallow serving bowls, if you prefer. Repeat with the remaining meringue.

In a mixing bowl, whisk the egg yolks with the remaining granulated sugar until thick and pale yellow. Whisking continuously, slowly pour in the milk used to poach the meringues, discarding the vanilla bean.

Transfer the custard mixture to the top half of a double boiler and cook, stirring continuously, until just thick enough to coat a spoon but still liquid and pourable. Remove from the heat and continue stirring for about 5 minutes more, until it begins to cool. Stir in the Sambuca.

Carefully pour the custard around—but not over—the meringue eggs on the platter to float them.

If you'd like the additional flourish of a garnish, melt the chocolate in a small pan over the double boiler. With a spoon, drizzle the melted chocolate back and forth over the meringue eggs and custard before serving.

Makes 6 servings

© Felicia Martinez/PhotoEdit

CHEESE

All some people need to complete a meal with total satisfaction is a select platter of cheeses—say a sharp Cheddar, a nutty Swiss or Grùyere, a creamy and tangy goat cheese, a rich and crumbly blue, a ripe and runny Brie—accompanied by assorted biscuits, a few slices of apple or pear, maybe some walnuts and, if they're really living it up, a small, ruby-red glass of aged port.

That certainly *is* an option for ending any meal in style. And all you have to do to serve it properly is patronize a market or deli with a good cheese department that lets you question and sample to come up with a selection of varied cheeses in prime condition. Keep the cheeses wrapped and stored in your fridge until just before meal time; then, as guests are seated for the first course, unwrap the cheeses and leave them on a platter to come to cool room temperature by the time you're ready to serve them.

This presentation is all well and good. But it ain't dessert.

Fortunately, you can have your cheese *and* dessert too—in the form of cheesecake.

Ricotta and Raisin Pie

This traditional Italian dessert is the original cheesecake, the prototype from which all others have evolved. Bake it at least several hours in advance—and up to 2 days ahead—so the cheesecake has time to chill.

Crust

2 cups all-purpose flour

1/2 teaspoon grated allspice

Pinch of salt

1/4 pound unsalted butter, chilled and cut into pieces

1/2 cup ice water

Filling

1/2 cup raisins

1/2 cup Marsala wine

1¹/₂ pounds ricotta cheese

1/2 cup sugar

1/2 cup crushed amaretti cookies

1 tablespoon grated orange zest

1 tablespoon grated lemon zest

4 eggs

For the crust, put the flour, allspice and salt in a food processor with the metal blade and pulse the machine 2 or 3 times to mix the ingredients. Add the butter and pulse the machine until the mixture resembles fine crumbs. Then, with the machine running, slowly pour in just enough ice water to bring the dough together into a ball that rides the blade. Roll out the dough and use it to line the bottom and sides of a 9-inch springform pan. Refrigerate for 1 hour.

Preheat the oven to 350°F.

For the filling, first put the raisins in a small bowl with the Marsala and leave them to soak for about 15 minutes.

Put the ricotta, sugar, amaretti cookies, orange and lemon zests and the eggs into the processor and pulse until smoothly blended. Drain the raisins thoroughly, then, with a rubber spatula, fold them into the ricotta mixture. Empty the filling into the chilled pastry shell and smooth its surface.

Bake the pie until its top is a light golden brown and a knife inserted into its center comes out clean, about 45 minutes. Cool to room temperature. Then refrigerate for at least 1 hour before serving. Cut into wedges.

Makes one 9-inch pie

© Steven Mark Needham/Envision

© Tom Campbell/FPG International

Brie Cheesecake

A good, creamy ripe Brie partially replaces the usual cream cheese in this variation on the classic American cheesecake, giving the dessert extra richness and a tangy edge. Since the recipe calls for Brie trimmed of all white rind, be sure to buy several ounces more than the ingredients list calls for.

The cheesecake may be made a day or two in advance.

To complement the Brie, serve slices of fresh apple alongside or on top of each slice of cheesecake.

Crust

1 cup graham cracker crumbs

1/2 cup finely chopped walnuts

6 tablespoons unsalted butter, melted

1/4 cup sugar

Filling

3/4 pound trimmed ripe Brie, at room temperature

3/4 pound cream cheese, at room temperature

3/4 cup sugar

4 eggs

1 egg yolk

1/2 cup heavy cream

1/2 cup sour cream

1 tablespoon lemon juice

1 tablespoon grated lemon zest

1/2 tablespoon vanilla extract

1 each red and green apples, for garnish

For the crust, stir together all the ingredients in a mixing bowl. Press them into the bottom and partially up the sides of a 9-inch springform pan. Refrigerate for 30 minutes.

Preheat the oven to 350°F.

For the filling, put the Brie, cream cheese and sugar in a food processor with the metal blade and pulse the machine to combine them. One at a time, pulse in the eggs, and then the egg yolk, until thoroughly blended. Then add the heavy cream, sour cream, lemon juice, zest and vanilla and process until smooth and thick.

Pour the filling into the prepared crust and bake on the center shelf of the oven for 45 minutes. Turn off the oven, leaving the door ajar, and let the cheesecake cool inside. Refrigerate the cheesecake.

Cut the cheesecake into wedges for serving. If you like, just before you serve it, core and slice the apples and place 2 or 3 alternating red and green slices on top or alongside each wedge of cheesecake.

Makes one 9-inch cheesecake

FLOURS AND GRAINS

From cakes to cookies, piecrusts to crêpes, flour is the very foundation of dessert making. Eggs may lighten it, milk moisten it, butter enrich it and sugar sweeten it; but without flour, in many cases there's just no dessert.

Throughout this book, you'll find recipes that call for flour. They all take the guesswork out of choosing which flour to use: Quite simply, buy your favorite brand of all-purpose flour. Specially milled and blended pastry flours may yield better results in the exacting recipes you'd find in a post-graduate course in the art of baking; and whole-wheat flours may contribute added fiber—and a tougher texture—to desserts with a decidedly sixties flair. But plain old all-purpose flour will do the job here just fine.

All of the recipes you'll find here and elsewhere that use flour get their defining character from ingredients other than the flour itself, which is content to be a sideline player, never taking the spotlight for itself.

Some of the most satisfying desserts of all, though, are those in which other grains take center stage. Hearty and filling, these rich puddings and crumbles speak of old-time goodness. It's not surprising that they've come to be included under the blanket label of "nursery food." While eating them, we all feel a little bit more comforted, protected and safe from harm.

English Nursery Rice Pudding

This rich, satisfying pudding is delicious served warm or chilled. For the former, you can prepare the ingredients and combine them in the casserole up to several hours in advance; then just start baking the pudding about an hour before serving. Or bake the pudding several hours or a day ahead, let it come to room temperature, then refrigerate it.

2 cups cooked white rice

2 cups half-and-half

2 eggs, lightly beaten

1/2 cup golden raisins

1/2 cup brown sugar

1/2 teaspoon grated lemon zest

1/2 teaspoon grated orange zest

1/2 teaspoon grated cinnamon

1/8 teaspoon grated nutmeg

1 cup heavy cream (optional)

1 cup strawberry jam (optional)

Preheat the oven to 350°F.

In a mixing bowl, stir together the rice, half-and-half, eggs, raisins, 1/3 cup of the sugar, lemon and orange zests and the spices.

Lightly butter a shallow 1½-quart baking dish and fill it with the pudding mixture. Evenly sprinkle the remaining sugar over the top.

Bake the pudding for 20 to 25 minutes, until hot and bubbly. Let cool slightly before serving it with a drizzle of heavy cream, if desired. Or cool to room temperature, refrigerate and serve cold in the English fashion, with a dollop of jam.

Makes 4 to 6 servings

© Steven Mark Needham/Envision

Indian Pudding

This traditional New England favorite, which gets its name not because it has Native American origins but because the early colonists called corn "Indian corn," combines cornmeal with molasses and maple syrup for a dessert so rich, thick and satisfying that it's perfect for a cold winter night. It's a slow-cooking dish that requires no advance preparation; bake it up and serve it hot from the oven.

6 cups milk

1 cup yellow cornmeal

1/4 cup molasses

1/4 cup pure maple syrup

1/4 cup brown sugar

1 teaspoon powdered ginger

1/2 teaspoon grated cinnamon

1/4 teaspoon baking soda

2 eggs, well beaten

1 quart vanilla ice cream (optional)

In a heavy saucepan, bring the milk almost to a boil.

Transfer the milk to the top half of a double boiler and slowly stir in the cornmeal. Cook over medium heat until the cornmeal begins to thicken, 15 to 20 minutes.

Preheat the oven to 250°F.

In a mixing bowl, stir in the molasses, maple syrup, sugar, ginger, cinnamon and baking soda. In a separate bowl, slowly stir about a cup of the cornmeal mixture into the eggs. Then stir the egg mixture back into the other ingredients, adding the remaining cooked cornmeal.

Generously butter a heavy 2-quart baking dish and pour in the pudding mixture. Bake for 2¹/₂ to 3 hours, until the pudding is thick enough to scoop and is covered with a thick brown crust.

Scoop into bowls and serve hot, with vanilla ice cream if you like.

Makes 6 to 8 servings

Cinnamon Apple Crumble with Oatmeal Topping

For most of us, the real appeal of baked crumbles is as much the crunchy grain-and-nut topping as the fruit that lies beneath it. You can assemble this crumble several hours ahead of time—in a larger casserole from which it can be scooped into serving bowls. If you like, substitute firm, ripe pears for the apples.

4 large, tart cooking apples

2 tablespoons lemon juice

2 teaspoons grated lemon zest

1 tablespoon ground cinnamon

1/2 cup raisins

1/2 cup coarsely chopped walnuts

1/2 cup honey, at room temperature

1/4 pound unsalted butter, melted

1 cup rolled oats

1/4 cup all-purpose flour

1/4 cup brown sugar

1/4 teaspoon allspice

1/4 teaspoon salt

1 pint vanilla ice cream or 1 cup heavy cream (optional)

Preheat the oven to 350°F.

Core the apples, peel them if you don't like the peels and toss them with the lemon juice. Spread them in the bottom of a generously buttered 1¹/₂-quart casserole, sprinkle evenly with the lemon zest and half the cinnamon and strew in the raisins and walnuts. Drizzle the honey evenly over the apples.

In a mixing bowl, stir together the butter, oats, flour, brown sugar, remaining cinnamon, allspice and salt. Crumble the mixture evenly over the apples.

Bake the crumble until the apples are tender and the topping crisp, about 45 minutes, covering the casserole with foil if it seems to be browning too quickly.

Serve hot, scooped into bowls and accompanied, if you like, by ice cream or a drizzle of heavy cream.

Makes 4 to 6 servings

© Burke/Triolo

FRUITS

They're the quintessential light dessert. And potentially the simplest: Just place a bowl or platter of perfect ripe seasonal fruits in the center of your table after dinner and all eyes go to them; all appetites are whetted for their fresh, clean, light tastes and textures.

These sublime qualities shine through in prepared desserts featuring fruit. Fruit pies and tarts display the best seasonal specimens. All manner of other preparations—from cakes to mousses, ice creams to soufflés, pies to crumbles—take advantage of the color and flavor of fruit at its best.

Fruit salads bring together two or more fresh fruits in harmonious combinations—highlighted, perhaps, by supplementary sweeteners and flavorings. Choose the elements with an eye toward color, flavor, texture and shape. Virtually all fruits combine in a pleasing composition of colors; but don't overwhelm the eye with too many different hues. Likewise, don't overwhelm the palate with so many flavors and textures that they blend together into a kind of gustatorial cacophony; two to four different fruits will provide variety without creating confusion. Cut up the fruits into shapes that are bite-size but reflect the natural shape of the fruit; remove the pith from citrus segments and, if you want to get very fancy, peel off the membranes from each segment; leave berries whole (except for strawberries, which should be sliced if they are larger than bite-size).

To some tastes, all a good fruit salad needs is a generous squeeze of lemon or lime. But you can go far beyond that with a light sprinkling of sugar for fruits that are tarter than average. A splash of a complementary fruit liqueur will throw the natural fruit flavors into sharper contrast.

Tropical Fruit Fantasy

The fruit salad can be made up to several hours in advance.

2 large ripe mangoes

2 ripe firm kiwis

2 navel oranges

1 small ripe pineapple

1/4 cup orange liqueur (Grand Marnier or Curacao)

Fresh mint sprigs

1/4 cup shredded coconut (optional)

With a small, sharp knife, carefully peel the mangoes. Cut off the flesh in 2 large slices from either side of each fruit's large, flat stone; cut each slice crosswise into bite-size pieces. Cut off the remaining flesh from each fruit in bite-size pieces. Put the fruit in a mixing bowl.

With the knife, peel the furry brown skin from the kiwis. Cut each kiwi's bright green flesh crosswise into 1/4-inch-thick slices. Add them to the mango.

Peel the oranges and separate them into segments, removing all the pith. If you like, peel the membranes from each segment. Cut each segment crosswise in half. Add to the bowl.

Peel the pineapple and core it with a coring knife or by cutting the fruit crosswise into several pieces and then carefully cutting out the core with a small, sharp knife. Cut the cored pineapple into 1/2-inch-thick slices, then cut each slice into bite-size wedges. Add them to the bowl.

Sprinkle the fruit with the liqueur and gently toss. Cover the bowl and refrigerate for at least 1 hour.

Arrange the fruit salad in a shallow serving bowl and garnish with mint sprigs. If your guests like, offer them shredded coconut to garnish their servings.

Makes 4 to 6 servings

© Steven Mark Needham/Envision

Berries Jubilee

One of the most extravagant of all dessert presentations is a fresh fruit compote, engulfed in a halo of flickering flames as it's ladled over rich ice cream. Cherries are the usual star of such an extravaganza. But this recipe takes advantage of firm, ripe, seasonal berries for a dazzling twist on tradition.

1¹/₂ quarts vanilla ice cream

1/3 cup framboise liqueur

1/2 cup sugar

1/2 cup water

3 tablespoons unsalted butter

3/4 cup small whole fresh strawberries, hulled

3/4 cup fresh raspberries

Scoop the ice cream into 6 heavy serving dishes and keep them chilled. Gently heat the framboise to lukewarm in the top half of double boiler.

In a medium saucepan, bring the sugar and water to a boil over medium-to-low heat. Swirl in the butter and simmer about 30 seconds more. Then add the berries and stir gently just to coat them with the syrup.

Set the dishes of ice cream on a serving tray. Ladle the fruit and syrup over the ice cream, and carefully spoon the warm framboise on top. Then, the instant before you carry the tray to the table, dim the dining room lights and use a long wooden matchstick to ignite the liqueur on each serving. Serve immediately.

Makes 6 servings

Fresh Mandarin Sherbet

The vibrant flavor of fresh mandarins—those tiny cousins of tangerines—is highlighted perfectly in this simple, light frozen dessert. You can make it a day or two ahead; but if it freezes too hard, be sure to allow time for it to soften to scooping consistency.

4 cups strained fresh mandarin juice

1 cup strained fresh lemon juice

1 cup sugar

2 teaspoons grated mandarin zest

1 teaspoon grated lemon zest

2 egg whites

In a heavy saucepan, bring the juices and sugar to a boil over medium heat, stirring continuously to dissolve the sugar. Then stir in the mandarin and lemon zests, remove from the heat and let cool to room temperature.

Transfer the mixture to a commercial ice-cream maker and start to freeze following manufacturer's directions. Meanwhile, beat the egg whites until they just begin to turn frothy and opaque. As soon as the sherbet mixture starts to turn thick and slushy, add the egg whites to it and continue mixing until frozen.

Makes 1/2 gallon

© Burke/Triolo

© FPG/International

NUTS AND DRIED FRUITS

There's something intensely satisfying about nuts and dried fruits. Just set them out together on a platter after dinner—pieces of fruit arrayed in rows like jewels; nutmeats, preshelled or still in their shells and accompanied by nutcrackers—and watch your guests as they compulsively eat them, morsel by morsel, until nothing remains.

The key to the appeal of dried fruits and nuts is, of course, their intensity. Shriveled in the sun or in ovens, dried fruits have the full flavor of fresh fruits, undiluted by water.

This intensity carries over into all kinds of desserts enhanced by nuts and dried fruits—bite-size confections, crunchy shards of nut brittle and cakes so dense with fruit or nuts that there's barely a need for flour.

Since a little bit of these ingredients goes a long way in most recipes, and since their prices are most reasonable when they're purchased in bulk, it's important to store dried fruits and nuts carefully. Keep dried fruits in an airtight container in a cool, dry place. Nuts, which have a high oil content and can go rancid, should be stored airtight at cool temperatures.

Hawaiian Dried Fruit and Nut Balls

Dried pineapple and papaya, chopped macadamia nuts and shredded coconut give these confections a distinctive tang and texture.

1 pound dried pineapple

1/2 pound dried papaya

1/4 pound dried apricots

1/4 cup honey

3/4 pound chopped macadamia nuts

1 cup shredded coconut

Put the pineapple, papaya and apricots in a food processor with the metal blade. Pulse the machine until they are coarsely chopped. Drizzle the honey over the chopped fruit in the processor; continue processing until finely chopped.

In a mixing bowl, stir the nuts into the chopped fruit until evenly blended.

Sprinkle the coconut on a work surface, and drop a generous tablespoon of the fruit-and-nut mixture into it. Roll the mixture in the coconut to coat it well and form a ball. Repeat with the rest of the mix. Put the balls on a sheet of wax paper to dry overnight at room temperature; then store packed between layers of wax paper or foil in airtight containers.

Makes 4¹/₂ dozen balls

© Burke/Triolo

Pine Nut Brittle

This variation on the classic peanut brittle features the most popular nut of two diverse cuisines, Italian and American Southwestern. Stored in layers separated by wax paper in an airtight container, the chunks of brittle will keep well for several weeks.

For a more elaborate confection, you can also dip individual bite-size pieces of the brittle into melted bittersweet chocolate, covering each piece only halfway. Let the dipped brittle set on wax paper before serving or storing.

1/4 pound unsalted butter, at room temperature

1 pound shelled pine nuts

1 cup granulated sugar

1 cup brown sugar

2/3 cup water

Preheat the oven to 300°F.

Generously butter a large marble slab or 2 large baking sheets. Set aside.

Fill the kitchen sink with several inches of cold water.

Spread the pine nuts evenly on a baking sheet and place them in the oven to roast until light golden, about 10 minutes. Watch them carefully to prevent burning, and remove them from the oven as soon as they begin to change color; they'll continue to darken outside of the oven.

Meanwhile, put the granulated and brown sugars and the water into a large heavy saucepan. Stir constantly over medium heat to dissolve the sugar; with a pastry brush dipped in water, wash down any sugar that sticks to the side of the pan.

As soon as all the sugar has dissolved, put a candy thermometer in the pan and raise the heat to high. Boil the syrup until it reaches about 325°F on the thermometer, then dip the bottom of the pan into the cold water in the sink.

Immediately add the warm pine nuts and gently stir them in. Then pour the mixture out onto the buttered surface and, with an oiled spatula, spread it out as thinly and evenly as you can, leaving the nuts in a single layer wherever possible.

When the brittle has cooled completely, break it into jagged pieces. Store in an airtight container.

Makes 2 pounds

Date Raisin Bars

Here is a recipe for classic dried fruit cookies. Stored airtight, they will keep well for a week or two.

Date and Raisin Filling

1/4 pound coarsely chopped pitted dates

1/4 pound seedless raisins

3/4 cup water

1/2 cup brown sugar

1/4 teaspoon salt

1/2 teaspoon almond extract

Butter Cookie Crust

2 cups all-purpose flour

1/2 cup granulated sugar

Pinch of salt

1/2 pound unsalted butter, chilled, cut into 1/2-inch pieces

Oat Crumble Topping

5 1/2 tablespoons unsalted butter, at room temperature

2/3 cup brown sugar

1/4 teaspoon vanilla extract

1 cup all-purpose flour

1/4 teaspoon salt

1/4 teaspoon baking soda

1 cup rolled oats

3 tablespoons water

For the filling, put the dates, raisins, water, sugar and salt in a medium saucepan and cook over low heat, stirring frequently, until the sugar dissolves completely and the mixture is thick and smooth. Remove from the heat and stir in the almond extract. Cool to room temperature.

Meanwhile, preheat the oven to 350°F.

For the cookie crust, put the flour, sugar and salt in a processor with the metal blade and pulse 2 or 3 times to blend. Add the butter and pulse the machine until the mixture resembles coarse crumbs. Remove the mixture to a lightly floured work surface and knead briefly, just until it forms a smooth dough.

Press the dough into an ungreased 15 1/2-by-10 1/2-by-1-inch jelly roll pan. Bake until lightly browned, about 15 minutes. Transfer the pan to a wire rack to cool for about 15 minutes.

Spread the filling evenly over the cookie crust.

Reduce the oven temperature to 325°F.

For the topping, cream together the butter, brown sugar and vanilla in a mixing bowl. In a separate bowl, stir together the flour, salt and baking soda; then stir them into the creamed mixture. Finally, stir in the oats and water to form a crumbly mixture.

With your fingers, crumble the topping evenly over the filling. Return the pan to the oven and bake until the topping is browned, about 30 minutes more.

Let the pan cool on a wire rack until the cookies are just warm to the touch. With a sharp knife, cut them into squares about 2 inches across; use a narrow spatula to transfer the squares to the wire rack to cool completely.

Store the cookies in an airtight container between layers of wax paper.

Makes 35 bars

Courtesy of Williams-Sonoma

Almond-Pistachio Cake with Amaretto Cream

This dense, moist cake is a variation on a French classic in which the pulverized crumbs of ladyfingers (available in most supermarkets) take the place of flour and form a subtle background for finely chopped nuts. All that's needed to complement the cake is lightly whipped cream with a little almond-flavored liqueur.

The cake may be baked several hours ahead of time. But it should be eaten well within 24 hours, to be enjoyed at its moistest.

20 ladyfingers

1/2 cup blanched almonds

1/2 cup blanched pistachios

1/2 teaspoon baking powder

2/3 cup sugar

5 tablespoons unsalted butter, at room temperature

1/4 teaspoon vanilla extract

3 eggs

2 tablespoons confectioners' sugar

1 cup heavy cream, chilled

2 tablespoons amaretto liqueur

In a food processor with the metal blade, process the ladyfingers until they form fine crumbs. Transfer to a mixing bowl.

Put the almonds in the processor, and pulse the machine until they are chopped to fine gravel-size pieces. Add them to the ladyfingers. Repeat with the pistachios. Add the baking powder and stir to mix.

In a separate bowl, cream together the sugar, butter and vanilla until smooth. Then stir in the eggs, one at a time, until thoroughly combined. Gradually stir the dry ingredients into this mixture to form a smooth batter.

Preheat the oven to 325°F.

Butter and flour a 9-inch round cake pan; line it with parchment paper or wax paper. Pour the batter into the pan. Bake until the cake is golden brown and its center springs back when touched, about 35 minutes.

Transfer the cake pan to a wire rack and let it cool. Unmold the cake onto a serving platter and remove the paper.

Dust the cake lightly with confectioners' sugar. If you'd like a decorative pattern, place a paper doily on top of the cake before you sugar it; then carefully lift off the doily.

Before serving the cake, lightly whip the cream just until it begins to thicken and increase in volume. Stir in the amaretto.

Serve the cake cut into wedges, with a generous dollop of cream.

Makes one 9-inch cake

CHOCOLATE

Chocolate brownies. Chocolate cake. Chocolate ice cream. Chocolate truffles and other chocolate-dipped confections. Hefty chunks of plain imported chocolate, right off the supermarket shelf. In any form, at any time, chocolate desserts hold an almost addictive fascination for the chocoholic—and the ordinary dessert lover also has to admit that they're mighty hard to pass up.

Oddly enough, this rich dessert flavoring is derived from the hard, bitter bean of the Latin American cacao tree; originally it was usually ground up and mixed with chiles and broth to make a thick, spicy beverage. The Spanish conquistador Cortez brought the bean home from Mexico, where he had been served the beverage by the Aztec king, before taking him prisoner and conquering his kingdom. Once in Spain, and sweetened up, chocolate became the in drink with the wealthy. But it wasn't until the nineteenth century that chocolate was finally incorporated into the realm of desserts and confections. Ingenious chefs have been making up for lost time ever since.

Chocolate as we know it has been substantially processed from its natural state, and an incredible variety of chocolate products is available. Sweetness levels may vary from bittersweet to semisweet. Milk or cream may have been added for a milder chocolate with smoother melting properties. Cocoa butter—the natural fat of the cacao bean—may have been added for a suaver consistency or taken away to make a harder, more brittle chocolate. The brown cocoa powder may even have been filtered away, and the cocoa butter mixed with cream, sugar and vanilla to make what's called white chocolate. All chocolate should be stored at cool room temperature—55° to 65°F—away from direct sunlight and heat sources.

While different recipes may call for chocolates with different properties, the final choice is a matter of taste. And what better invitation does a chocoholic need to sit down to a serious comparative study?

Chocolate Hazelnut Truffles

So named for its resemblance to the prized fungus, the chocolate truffle is itself the epitome of chocolate confections—fine chocolate melted with rich cream, discreetly flavored, then rolled in cocoa powder (which resembles the earth that clings to the other kind of truffles).

Use the following recipe as your model for making all kinds of truffles to suit your fancy. Substitute another liqueur for the Frangelico, if you like. Or place a piece of candied fruit or a whole small berry inside each truffle instead of the hazelnut. Roll them in coconut or crushed nuts instead of the cocoa; or dip them in melted chocolate.

Keep the truffles in an airtight box at cool room temperature, and eat them within 2 or 3 days of making them. (This last step should pose no problem at all.)

3 dozen whole hazelnuts

10 ounces semisweet chocolate, broken into pieces

1/2 cup heavy cream

2 tablespoons hazelnut liqueur (Frangelico)

1/2 cup unsweetened cocoa powder

1/4 cup confectioners' sugar

Preheat the oven to 325°F.

Spread the hazelnuts on a baking sheet, and toast them in the oven for about 10 minutes. Let them cool slightly, then carefully rub them between dry kitchen towels to remove their skins. Set the nuts aside.

Put the chocolate and cream in the top of a double boiler over gently simmering water. Stir continuously as the chocolate melts, until it is completely blended with the cream.

Remove the mixture from the heat, and pour it into a mixing bowl. Let the mixture cool and thicken, stirring occasionally; when it is just slightly warm and fairly thick but still stirable, mix in the Frangelico. Cover and let cool to room temperature, until the mixture is very thick but pliable.

Stir together the cocoa and sugar, and sprinkle the mixture evenly on a large plate.

With a teaspoon, scoop up generous balls of the mixture. Press a toasted hazelnut into the center of each ball, then roll them with your fingers in the cocoa-sugar mixture to coat evenly.

Pop each coated truffle into a small paper candy cup. Chill in the refrigerator until hard, then store at cool room temperature.

Makes 3 dozen

Chocolate-Dipped Fruits and Nuts

These delightful chocolate-coated nibbles are perfect served with good coffee. White chocolate has a pristine beauty and subtle flavor that complements fresh or candied fruit nicely, while the earthy flavor of nuts seems to go better with dark or milk chocolate. Buy the best quality dipping chocolate—dark, milk or white—you can find. You're free, of course, to dip the fruits in regular chocolate and the nuts in white, if you wish.

It's best to prepare the confections no more than a few hours before serving; the high water content of the fruit will eventually spoil the evenness of the coating.

1/2 pound white chocolate, broken into pieces

1/2 pound semisweet or milk chocolate, broken into pieces

6 medium-size strawberries, with stems attached

12 (1-inch) chunks candied pineapple

12 firm ripe cherries, pitted, stems left attached if possible

12 large Brazil nuts

12 walnut halves

18 jumbo roasted almonds

Put the white chocolate and the semisweet or dark chocolate in separate metal bowls that will rest inside the rim of a medium saucepan.

Fill the saucepan with water and bring it to a boil. Reduce the heat to a simmer and, resting the bowl of white chocolate inside the pan, melt the chocolate, stirring frequently.

Hold the strawberries by the stem and dip them one at a time into the melted white chocolate, turning to coat about two-thirds of each berry, leaving only the broad stem ends uncoated. As each berry is dipped, place it on wax paper to cool and set.

Use a thin skewer or toothpick to pick up each chunk of pineapple, dipping it about two-thirds of the way into the melted chocolate. Then place each dipped piece on wax paper.

Holding the cherries by their stems, dip them 2 at a time, side-by-side, into the chocolate, covering all but the tiniest bit of their stem ends. Set the double clusters of dipped cherries on the wax paper, making sure the 2 cherries touch so they'll set together.

Melt the semisweet or milk chocolate. With a fork, dip the Brazil nuts individually, lifting them out and easing them onto the wax paper. Repeat with the walnuts. Finally, put all the almonds into the remaining melted chocolate and, with a teaspoon, remove 3 at a time, easing them onto the wax paper to set as a cluster.

When the chocolate has set on the dipped fruits and nuts, place them in individual candy cups or on a doily-lined platter. Store in a cool place until serving.

Makes 6 servings

© Thomas Lindley/FPG International

Chocolate Chip Brownie Hot Fudge Ice Cream Pie

Yes, you read it right. This could be the ultimate chocolate dessert. You could prepare and enjoy each element of this recipe separately, but why bother to hold back?

You can make the ice cream, bake the brownie and layer them together the night before you plan to serve the dessert. The hot fudge sauce may be made in just a few minutes right before serving time, or you can make it in advance, refrigerate it and reheat it before serving.

If you want to get extra indulgent, you can press a layer of your favorite chocolate or chocolate-coated candy bar—broken or cut into pieces—into the top of the ice cream. Try Heath Bars, Snickers, Mr. Goodbars, Nestle's Crunches, Reese's Peanut Butter Cups or whatever else strikes your fancy.

And if you want to make the dessert even easier, just bake the brownie from scratch and use your favorite brands of ice cream and hot fudge sauce.

Extra-Chocolate Ice Cream

1 pint half-and-half

1²/₃ cups sugar

1 cup unsweetened cocoa powder

8 egg yolks

2 ounces unsweetened cooking chocolate, grated

1 quart whipping cream

1/2 tablespoon vanilla extract

Chocolate Chip Brownie

1¹/₄ sticks (10 tablespoons) unsalted butter

1 cup sugar

3/4 cup all-purpose flour

1/2 cup unsweetened cocoa powder

1/2 teaspoon salt

1/2 teaspoon baking powder

2 eggs

2 tablespoons corn syrup

3/4 teaspoon vanilla extract

1/2 teaspoon almond extract

3/4 cup bittersweet chocolate chips

Creamy Hot Fudge Sauce

1¹/₂ cups heavy cream

1¹/₂ cups sugar

1/4 teaspoon salt

3 ounces unsweetened cooking chocolate, grated

4 tablespoons unsalted butter, cut into pieces

1/2 tablespoon vanilla extract

1/2 teaspoon coffee extract

For the ice cream, put the half-and-half, sugar, cocoa and egg yolks in a processor or blender; pulse several times, then process until smoothly blended.

Transfer the mixture to a heavy saucepan and add the grated chocolate. Cook over very low heat, stirring continuously, until the chocolate melts and the mixture just begins to bubble around the edges.

Pour the mixture into a bowl and refrigerate it until cold. Then stir in the whipping cream and vanilla and freeze in a commercial ice-cream maker, following manufacturer's directions.

Meanwhile, for the brownie, preheat the oven to 350°F. Butter the bottom and halfway up the sides of a 9-inch circular springform pan.

In a mixing bowl, cream together the butter and sugar. In a separate bowl, stir together the flour, cocoa, salt and baking powder. In a third bowl, beat together the eggs, corn syrup and vanilla and almond extracts until smooth.

Gradually stir the flour mixture into the creamed mixture. Then stir in the egg mixture until well blended. Finally, fold in the chocolate chips.

Pour the mixture into the springform pan, smoothing the surface. Bake just until the edge of the brownie turns firm but the center is still soft and springy, about 40 minutes.

Remove from the oven and place the pan on a wire rack to cool. Do not remove the side from the pan.

When the brownie is cool and the ice cream is done (but still fairly soft), spread the ice cream evenly inside the pan on top of the brownie. Cover with foil and transfer to the freezer.

Thirty minutes before you plan to serve the dessert, remove the pan from the freezer and let it sit at room temperature so the ice cream softens slightly.

Meanwhile, prepare the hot fudge sauce (you can also prepare it in advance and reheat it in the top of a double boiler a few minutes before serving). For the sauce, put the cream, sugar, salt and chocolate in a heavy saucepan and cook over medium heat, stirring frequently until the sugar dissolves and the chocolate melts completely. Stir in the butter until it melts, reduce the heat slightly, and continue cooking, stirring occasionally, until the sauce is thick, 5 to 7 minutes. Stir in the vanilla and coffee extracts.

Wrap a hot, damp towel around the side of the springform pan to loosen it, and remove the side. Cut the pie into wedges and pour the hot fudge sauce generously over each serving.

Makes 6 to 8 servings

© Steven Mark Needham/Envision

SUGAR AND OTHER SWEETENERS

"Sugar," wrote the celebrated nineteenth-century French epicure Jean-Anthelme Brillat-Savarin in his masterwork *The Physiology of Taste*, "harms nothing but the purse." It's clear that the great gourmand was recognizing a simple fact that's as true today as it has been throughout time: People just can't get enough sweets.

The word *candy* has as its root the Arabic *qand*, which means sugar. From caramels to fudge, nougats to toffee, classic candies are made primarily from sugar—or its relatives—manipulated by the confectioner in various ways. Some of those techniques call for skills and equipment beyond the scope of most home cooks; but many more candies are easily made with the assistance of little more than a candy thermometer (available in any well-stocked cookware store) and some good, heavy saucepans for cooking the sugar syrups evenly.

The range of other natural sweeteners beyond common granulated sugar expands your dessert repertoire even more. Molasses, the thick, syrupy residue from the sugar-making process, has a deep, earthy taste that's perfect for old-fashioned desserts. Brown sugar—which is simply sugar in which some molasses content remains—has a rich, mellow flavor that makes it an interesting substitute for regular sugar in certain recipes. Maple syrup, from the sap of the maple tree, has an incomparably distinctive taste. And honey has a homey quality that actually seems to *comfort* the tastebuds as it delights them with sweetness.

Granulated sugars absorb moisture easily, becoming hard and solid, while syrups exposed to air tend to evaporate and crystallize. So keep sugars and other sweeteners in a dry airtight container at cool room temperature.

Maple and Brown Sugar Walnut Fudge

The mellow flavors of maple syrup, brown sugar and walnuts combine beautifully. The smooth, creamy texture of this classic fudge is a result of letting the mixture cool and form small crystals before it is beaten and thickened. If you prefer a somewhat harder, more grainy style of fudge, beat the syrup as soon as it's done cooking; this will cause larger sugar crystals to form.

Of course, if you like you can leave the nuts out or add other varieties. Or, for an outrageous fudge, replace half of the walnuts with chocolate chips.

You can make the fudge in advance. It keeps well in the refrigerator for several weeks if stored in an airtight container; and it freezes well for several months.

2 cups granulated sugar

1 cup brown sugar

3/4 cup pure maple syrup

1 cup milk

1/2 cup half-and-half

3 tablespoons light corn syrup

1/4 teaspoon salt

4 tablespoons unsalted butter, cut into 1/2-inch pieces, at room temperature

1 teaspoon vanilla extract

1 cup coarsely chopped walnuts

In a large heavy saucepan, stir together the sugars, maple syrup, milk, half-and-half, corn syrup and salt. Put the pan over medium to low heat and cook, stirring constantly, until the sugar dissolves completely.

Put a sugar thermometer in the pan and leave the pan on the heat, without stirring, until the mixture reaches 238°F. Meanwhile, fill the kitchen sink with several inches of cold water. As soon as the mixture reaches the desired temperature, immediately remove the pan from the heat and dip its bottom in the cold water. Then put the pan aside at cool room temperature until the mixture is lukewarm.

Lightly oil an 8-inch-square baking pan, or spray it with nonstick cooking spray.

Add the butter and vanilla to the saucepan and, with a wooden spoon, stir and beat the fudge mixture until it no longer looks glossy and is thick and creamy. Stir in the nuts and immediately spread the mixture in the baking pan. Let the fudge cool completely, then use a knife to cut it into 1-inch squares. Place the squares in individual candy cups, or stack them in single layers separated by wax paper, and store in an airtight container at cool room temperature.

Makes 64 pieces

© Steven Mark Needham/Envision

Honey-Nut Nougat

Add a sweet honey-and-sugar syrup to beaten egg white, stir in lots of nuts, and you get one of the world's most satisfying confections—nougat.

You can use any combination of nuts you like. And, for an Italian twist, you can also add candied orange or lemon peel. For a Middle Eastern taste, stir a few teaspoons of orange flower water or rose water into the mixture with the nuts.

To keep these sticky treats manageable when you serve them, you sandwich the nougat mixture between sheets of edible rice paper, which you can find in a well-stocked gourmet shop, a candy-making supply store (check your telephone directory) or an Asian market.

The nougat will keep fresh for up to a week if stored airtight in a cool, dry place.

2 sheets edible rice paper, trimmed to 8-by-10-inches each

1/2 pound hazelnuts

1/2 pound blanched whole almonds

1/2 cup honey

1 cup granulated sugar

1/2 cup water

2 egg whites, stiffly beaten

1/2 teaspoon almond extract

1/2 teaspoon vanilla extract

Lightly grease an 8-by-10-inch baking pan, or spray it with nonstick coating spray, and line the bottom with a sheet of rice paper. Set aside.

Preheat the oven to 325°F. Spread the hazelnuts and the almonds on 2 separate baking sheets, and toast them in the oven for about 10 minutes. Set the almonds aside, covering the baking sheet with heavy aluminum foil to keep them warm. Let the hazelnuts cool slightly, then carefully rub them between dry kitchen towels to remove their skins. Set the nuts aside on their baking sheet, covering them with heavy aluminum foil to keep them warm.

Fill the kitchen sink with several inches of cold water.

Put the honey in a small saucepan, and warm it over low heat just until it becomes fairly liquid and pourable.

Put the sugar and water in a large heavy saucepan, and stir over medium heat until the sugar dissolves. Add a candy thermometer, bring to a boil and continue boiling until the syrup reaches about 280°F. Pour in the warm honey and boil until the syrup reaches 290°F. Briefly dip the bottom of the pan in cold water.

Beating continuously with a wire whisk, slowly pour the syrup into the beaten egg whites until fully incorporated. Stir in the warm nuts and the almond and vanilla extracts.

Immediately empty the mixture into the prepared pan, packing it down and smoothing its surface. Place another sheet of rice paper on top. Place another pan of the same size, or a small board that fits the pan, inside and put kitchen weights or several large cans of food on top to weight down the nougat.

After about 3 hours, when the nougat has completely cooled and set, unmold it and carefully cut it into 1-by-2-inch strips with a sharp, heavy knife. If you like, wrap each individual piece in a twist of cellophane; or just stack them in single layers between sheets of wax paper in a container. Store airtight in a cool, dry place.

Makes 40 pieces

Caramel Butterscotch Sauce

This is a classic ice cream sauce, enhanced with the rich flavors of caramelized sugar syrup, butter and half-and-half. If you like, you can add chopped pecans or walnuts.

You can make this sauce in advance and store it in a jar in the refrigerator, to be served cold or gently reheated.

1/2 cup granulated sugar

1/2 cup water

1 cup packed dark brown sugar

1/4 cup dark corn syrup

6 tablespoons unsalted butter

1/4 cup half-and-half

Fill the kitchen sink with several inches of cold water.

In a small, white enameled saucepan, combine the granulated sugar with 2 tablespoons of the water. Cook over high heat until the sugar melts and turns a light golden caramel color. Immediately remove from the heat, and dip the bottom of the pan in the cold water. Then set the pan aside and leave it undisturbed.

Put the brown sugar, corn syrup, butter and half-and-half in a large heavy saucepan. Bring to a boil over medium to low heat, stirring until the sugar dissolves. Put a candy thermometer in the pan and continue boiling, stirring occasionally, until the mixture reaches 234–238°F, 3 to 4 minutes.

Remove the pan from the heat, and briefly dip its bottom in cold water. Set it aside.

Add the remaining water to the pan of caramelized sugar and, over medium heat, stir just until the caramel dissolves completely. Immediately stir the caramel into the other ingredients.

Serve the hot sauce at once. Or let it cool and refrigerate it in a covered jar. The sauce can then be served cold; or gently reheat it by placing the jar, uncovered, in a saucepan filled with cold water and then bringing the water to a simmer over medium to low heat.

Makes 1¹/₂ cups

© Gordon E. Smith

GELATIN

A dessert of fresh fruit juice holds a miraculous shape, sparkling like a jewel. An airy mixture of sweetened and flavored cream seems so light and smooth it could almost float away.

Some kind of kitchen magic is going on in such ethereal desserts. And the trick is gelatin.

A natural extract of the protein collagen, gelatin is used as a setting agent in some of the dessert kitchen's most delicate creations. Dried and powdered gelatin is dissolved in liquid and mixed with the remaining dessert ingredients. Just a few spoonfuls are sufficient to set several cups of liquid. Products from different manufacturers may vary somewhat in strength, so it's always a good idea to check the package's suggested proportions of gelatin to liquid before embarking on any specific recipe.

Note: *Don't improvise any gelatin desserts of your own that include fresh pineapple or papaya; both these tropical fruits contain an enzyme that prevents gelatin from setting. Heat, however, breaks down that enzyme, so it's okay to make a gelatin dessert with cooked or canned papaya or pineapple.*

Mandarin Orange Gelatin with Fresh Raspberries

The combination of sparkling orange gelatin and bright red raspberries makes for a particularly beautiful dessert. Use the juice of fresh mandarins, those small, sweet cousins of the orange and tangerine. If they aren't available, you can substitute tangerines or oranges. Fresh raspberries are preferable, but you can substitute sliced strawberries.

Allow at least 4 hours for the gelatin to set completely. You may want to make the dessert the night before you plan to serve it. For this recipe you'll need a cheesecloth.

2 1/4 cups cold water

1 3/4 cups sugar

4 tablespoons unflavored powdered gelatin

3 tablespoons fresh lemon juice, strained through a double thickness of cheesecloth

4 egg whites, lightly beaten

1 3/4 cups fresh mandarin juice, strained through a double thickness of cheesecloth

3/4 cup whole fresh raspberries

2 cups heavy cream, whipped to soft peaks and chilled

In a heavy saucepan, stir together the water, sugar, gelatin and lemon juice. Continue stirring over low heat until the sugar and gelatin dissolve; raise the heat slightly and continue cooking until the liquid barely begins to simmer. Remove the pan from the heat, cover and let the mixture sit for about 30 minutes.

Rapidly whisk in the egg whites; then return the pan to low heat and whisk gently but continuously until a foam of egg whites forms on the surface. Pour the contents of the pan through a strainer lined with double cheesecloth into a 1 1/2- to 2-quart glass bowl.

Stir the mandarin juice into the strained liquid. Ladle about a quarter of the mixture into a 5-cup gelatin mold, and put it in the refrigerator to chill until fairly set, about 2 hours. Meanwhile, keep the remainder covered at room temperature.

Arrange the raspberries decoratively on top of the layer of set gelatin. Ladle the remaining gelatin mixture over the berries to fill the mold. Return the mold to the refrigerator to set for at least 2 hours more.

To unmold the gelatin, fill the kitchen sink with warm water. Run the tip of a small, sharp knife around the edge of the mold. Then dip the mold into the water up to its rim. Place a serving platter upside down over the mold; holding the two together, turn them over, then carefully lift off the mold.

Dish up the gelatin with a large serving spoon or a cake slicer. Garnish with whipped cream.

Makes 6 to 8 servings

Key Lime Mousse

Gelatin is the special setting agent in this elegant variation on the classic Florida pie. If you can't find the small, yellow-green, thin-skinned Key limes, substitute regular limes.

Prepare the dessert at least several hours ahead to allow time for it to chill and set. You can make it up to a day ahead.

1 tablespoon unflavored powdered gelatin

1/2 cup warm water

3/4 cup Key lime juice (6 to 8 whole limes, reserve one whole lime to use as garnish)

1 tablespoon finely grated Key lime zest

6 eggs

1¹/2 cups granulated sugar

1/4 teaspoon salt

2 cups whipping cream

12 honey graham crackers, crushed into fine crumbs

1 tablespoon confectioners' sugar

1/2 teaspoon vanilla extract

In a mixing bowl, soak the gelatin in the warm water until it softens and dissolves, stirring occasionally, about 5 minutes.

Gradually stir the lime juice and zest into the gelatin. Set the mixture aside.

In the large bowl of an electric beater, beat the eggs with the sugar and salt at high speed until very thick and foamy, 7 to 10 minutes. Reduce the speed to low and gradually beat in the Key lime mixture.

Cover the bowl and refrigerate just until the mixture begins to set but is still fairly liquid, about 1 hour.

Whip half the cream until it forms soft peaks. Fold it into the Key lime mixture.

Spoon the mixture into 8 individual glass dessert bowls, filling them halfway. Sprinkle a generous layer of crushed graham crackers in each bowl, reserving about 3 tablespoons. Then fill with the remaining Key lime mixture. Refrigerate for at least 2 hours.

Before serving, whip the remaining cream with the confectioners' sugar and vanilla until it forms fairly firm peaks. Pipe or spoon the cream decoratively over each serving and sprinkle with some crushed graham crackers. For the final garnish, thinly slice a Key lime, then cut each slice two thirds of the way across its diameter, then twist the slice and place it on top of a serving.

Makes 8 servings

Fondue Party

*M*ost people think of fondue as the traditional Swiss dish of melted cheese served with cubes of bread for dipping. But the word fondue *has nothing to do with cheese; it actually means melted, and also applies to another Swiss culinary tradition, one of the most delightful desserts imaginable.*

In this case, the melted ingredient is chocolate—Swiss chocolate, of course. It becomes the centerpiece for a profusion of sweet dippables—fresh fruit, dried fruit, nuts, cubes of cake and anything else that strikes your fancy.

The informal fun and easy preparation of a fondue party makes it perfect for casual, late-night entertaining. The fondue mixture is easily assembled and melts in less than half an hour. Your only advance preparation is cleaning the fruit and cutting it up into bite-size pieces along with the other ingredients—including the best-quality pound cake and other baked dippables you can find.

The melted chocolate mixture itself goes into a traditional fondue pot, or any other heavy, heatproof vessel that can sit over a small tabletop flame. Set out long forks, or just an assortment of attractive long toothpicks for dipping, along with spoons that guests can use to fish out any bites that drop into the pot.

M E N U

Swiss Chocolate Fondue

Fresh Seasonal Fruits

Pound Cake, Angel Food Cake and Assorted Cookies

Dried Fruits and Nuts

Coffee and Liqueurs

For 10 to 12 people

Swiss Chocolate Fondue

Use your favorite, best-quality brand of imported Swiss chocolate for this recipe.

A dash of raspberry liqueur—framboise—heightens the flavor. Feel free to substitute any other liqueur you like, such as Grand Marnier or crème de cacao or any of the many brands of coffee-flavored liqueur; or use whiskey, bourbon or rum instead. For even greater variety, divide the recipe into 2 or 3 batches and flavor each one differently, serving them in separate fondue pots for guests to sample and compare.

The fondue mixture takes less than half an hour to prepare. If you like, you can make it an hour or more in advance and keep it at room temperature; reheat on top of a double boiler and stir in the liqueur just before serving.

Any leftovers make an excellent ice cream topping.

1/2 pound unsweetened chocolate, broken into small pieces

1/2 pound semisweet chocolate, broken into small pieces

2 1/2 cups superfine sugar

2 cups heavy cream

3/4 cup (1¹/2 sticks) unsalted butter, cut into 1/2-inch cubes

1/4 teaspoon salt

2/3 cup framboise (raspberry liqueur)

Put the chocolate, sugar, cream, butter and salt in the top of a double boiler over barely simmering water. Cook, stirring frequently, until the chocolate and butter have melted and the sugar has dissolved completely, 10 to 12 minutes. Stir in the framboise until thoroughly blended.

Transfer the mixture to a fondue pot and serve immediately. Or hold the mixture, covered, at room temperature and gently reheat over the double boiler before serving with assorted dippables.

Makes 10 to 12 servings

Fresh Seasonal Fruits

Allow at least 1/2 cup of fresh fruit per guest.

Strawberries are a superb choice, and you can leave their stems on as convenient dipping handles. Other seasonal berries also work well. But be sure to get fruit that's not only ripe but also firm, so it doesn't disintegrate when dipped.

Bananas, cut into bite-size chunks, go splendidly with chocolate, as do wedges of apple. Since both these fruits tend to oxidize and discolor, cut them up just minutes before serving, and keep a fresh supply coming as the party progresses.

A surprisingly good dippable is firm, ripe cantaloupe or honeydew melon. You might be skeptical the first time you serve them with a chocolate fondue, but one bite and you will be hooked.

Pound Cake, Angel Food Cake and Assorted Cookies

Go to the local gourmet shop or bakery with the best selection of cakes and cookies and buy an elegant assortment for dipping.

Good, firm pound cake and angel food cake are excellent candidates for fondue. Cut them into 1- to 1¹/2-inch squares, and arrange them on a tray beside the fondue pot.

Fairly plain but flavorful cookies are also good dipping choices. Choose those with a shape that lends itself to dunking by hand; ladyfingers, Jewish mandelbrot and Italian almond biscotti are all appropriate.

One 10- to 12-inch loaf-shaped pound cake and 1 small ring-shaped angel food cake should be more than sufficient. Figure on an average of 2 or 3 cookies per guest.

Dried Fruits and Nuts

Arrange a tray of other small, sweet treats for your guests to dip.

You can use all kinds of dried or glacé fruits—apricots, pineapple chunks, peaches, pears, papaya spears and so on.

Nuts are delicious additions, too, though they do pose a problem: How do you keep from losing them in the pot? Walnut and pecan halves are fairly easy to impale on the sharp ends of fondue forks. For other kinds of nuts, you might want to offer the option of long, sundae spoons.

In all, allow about 1¹/2 to 2 cups of assorted fruits and nuts for each person.

Create-a-
Crêpe Party

*A*t an informal party, guests love to participate in the cooking—provided, of course, that you've done most of the preparation beforehand.

This sophisticated yet casual dessert party, suitable as much for a weekend afternoon as an after-dinner event, centers on do-it-yourself crêpes —a light, French-style pancake that guests can cook themselves at the kitchen stove or over a tabletop burner. Accompanying the crêpes are several toppings and fillings, such as ice cream fudge sauces.

You can prepare the crêpe batter, the fillings and the sauces several hours or up to a day or two ahead of time. If your kitchen isn't big enough to handle the crush of people, check with a rental company to see about getting tabletop burners with stands or grids to support the crêpe pans.

The pans themselves are fairly standard items in most good cookware stores. You'll want 7-inch-diameter crêpe pans, preferably of cast iron (though you may prefer good, heavy crêpe pans with a nonstick coating).

Bearing the crêpe's native land in mind, you may want to decorate in French country style—floral prints, heavy earthenware, dazzling white porcelain, jugs of fresh flowers and so on. Put Edith Piaf or Jacques Brel on the stereo and, voila! Your party is ready to begin.

M E N U

Classic French Crêpes à l'Orange

Berries Jubilee

Suzette Topping

French Vanilla Ice Cream

Creamy Hot Fudge Sauce

Wet Walnut Sauce

For 8 to 10 people

Classic French Crêpes a l'Orange

This traditional crêpe batter is embellished with a hint of orange-flavored liqueur; use either Cointreau, Grand Marnier or Curacao.

You can make the batter as late as an hour in advance, or up to 3 days ahead of time.

Demonstrate a crêpe or two to your guests before turning them loose. Be sure to keep an eye on the tabletop burners, to ensure that the heat is adjusted correctly and that they remain stable on your serving table.

If you have any leftover batter, make crêpes with it the following day. Stack the crêpes between sheets of wax paper and then wrap them securely in airtight freezer bags; store in the freezer, where they'll keep for several months. Defrost in the refrigerator before using.

2 cups all-purpose flour

1/8 teaspoon salt

5 eggs, lightly beaten

2 1/2 cups milk

1 tablespoon plus 2 teaspoons orange-flavored liqueur

1/4 cup unsalted butter, melted

Put the flour and salt in a mixing bowl and make a well in the center. Add the eggs and 2 cups of the milk, and stir gently from the center outwards with a wire whisk to combine the ingredients; then beat to make a smooth batter. Stir in the liqueur and 1 tablespoon plus 1 teaspoon of the melted butter.

Cover the bowl and set it aside at room temperature for about 1 hour. Pour the batter through a wire mesh strainer to remove any lumps. Transfer the batter to a measuring cup, or place a 1-ounce ladle inside the bowl.

Over low to medium heat, heat a little butter in each of the 7-inch crêpe pans you or your guests are using. Pour off the butter, reserving it in a small container, to leave just an even gloss inside each pan.

Pour or ladle a generous 1 ounce of batter into each crêpe pan. Quickly swirl the pan to coat the bottom evenly, then immediately pour any excess batter back into the bowl.

Cook the crêpe until its surface is covered with bubbles, about 1 minute. Then, with a narrow spatula, gently flip the crêpe over and cook about 1 minute more.

Serve immediately with a choice of fillings or toppings.

Note: *To season a new cast-iron crêpe pan that's never been used, fill it with inexpensive, flavorless vegetable oil and carefully heat it on a back burner of your stove until the oil is almost smoking. Then turn off the flame and let the pan cool and sit for 24 hours before discarding the oil and thoroughly wiping down the pan with paper towels. Never wash a crêpe pan after cooking; all you need to do is wipe it clean with paper towels.*

Makes about 3 dozen crêpes

Berries Jubilee

Fresh berries, gently warmed in syrup, are another excellent crêpe topping or filling.

Prepare a double batch of the Berries Jubilee recipe on page 48. Instead of flambeing the berries, carefully and gently swirl the framboise liqueur into the mixture away from the heat, immediately after adding the berries.

Spoon the Berries Jubilee into freshly made crêpes, with or without ice cream, then roll them up and dust with confectioners' sugar.

© Michael Grand

Suzette Topping

Crêpes Suzette is without a doubt the most famous French crêpe dessert, made by flambéing the crêpes in a buttery, brandied syrup.

Tabletop flambéing by your guests is definitely *not* recommended, or you'll spend most of your party worrying rather than enjoying yourself. Instead, this topping captures all the flavor of classic crêpes Suzette, without setting fire to anything. Set it out on the table with a small ladle, for guests to pour over their freshly made crêpes that are plain or ice cream filled.

Keep the topping warm in a chafing dish, on a hot plate or over a tabletop warmer. You can prepare it several hours in advance, store it in the refrigerator and gently reheat it before guests arrive.

1 cup thin-shred orange marmalade

1/2 cup unsalted butter, cut into pieces

1/3 cup brandy or cognac

1/4 cup orange-flavored liqueur

Confectioners' sugar

Put the marmalade, butter, brandy and liqueur in a saucepan over low heat. Cook, stirring frequently, until the marmalade and butter have melted and the ingredients are completely blended.

Spoon a few tablespoons of the topping over one or more freshly cooked crêpes. Then fold the crêpes in halves or quarters and dust with confectioners' sugar.

Makes about 2 cups

French Vanilla Ice Cream

A scoop of soft, cold, freshly churned ice cream is heavenly when rolled up inside a hot crêpe. You can embellish it with either the berry or the Suzette mixture or add hot fudge or, for that matter, go hog-wild with any combination of the above.

Of course, you don't have to make your own ice cream. Feel free to buy your favorite premium brand of vanilla. Just be sure that, homemade or store-bought, the ice cream is allowed to soften at room temperature—about 30 minutes before serving—to reach a scoopable consistency that will melt slightly when rolled in the crêpe.

This ice cream recipe will stay in peak serving condition for up to a week.

1 quart half-and-half

2 teaspoons vanilla extract

3 whole eggs

3 egg yolks

1 cup sugar

In a heavy saucepan over medium heat, warm the half-and-half just until bubbles appear around the edge of the pan. Stir in the vanilla extract.

In a mixing bowl, beat together the eggs, egg yolks and sugar with a wire whisk until the mixture is thick, pale and frothy, 3 to 5 minutes. Whisking continuously, gradually pour the cream into the egg mixture.

Return the mixture to the saucepan and stir over very low heat just until it is thick enough to coat a spoon, 3 to 5 minutes. Remove from the heat, and set the bottom of the pan inside a baking pan filled with ice and water. Continue stirring the mixture until it cools to room temperature.

Freeze the mixture in an ice-cream maker, following manufacturer's directions. Serve immediately. Or transfer to the freezer to harden, allowing the ice cream to sit at room temperature for about 30 minutes before scooping.

Makes about 1/2 gallon

Creamy Hot Fudge Sauce

Prepare a batch of the Creamy Hot Fudge Sauce that appears as part of the recipe for Chocolate Chip Brownie Hot Fudge Ice Cream Pie (page 61). Keep it warm in a chafing dish or on a hot plate, to be ladled over plain, ice cream–filled or fruit–topped crêpes.

Wet Walnut Sauce

This favorite soda fountain sundae topping is excellent spooned over ice cream–filled or plain crêpes.

You can make it several hours in advance or up to 2 days ahead, storing it covered in the refrigerator. Gently reheat before serving and keep warm in a chafing dish or on a hot plate.

1 cup packed brown sugar

1/2 cup unsalted butter, cut into pieces

1/2 cup half-and-half

Pinch of salt

1 1/2 cups broken walnut pieces

In a medium saucepan over low heat, melt the sugar and butter, stirring occasionally.

Pour in the half-and-half and, stirring frequently, continue cooking just until tiny bubbles begin to form around the edge of the mixture, 3 to 5 minutes. Stir in the softened walnuts.

Makes 3 cups

Light Summer
Indulgences

No, "light dessert" isn't an oxymoron.

Dessert doesn't necessarily have to be a calorie- and fat-laden course, and a dessert party can be easily targeted to the tastes of the health-conscious and dieters. The key, of course, is to concentrate on fresh fruits and other light, low-calorie ingredients, and avoid ingredients like egg yolks and cream.

Your conscience can remain clear when you invite friends over for the following menu. It's ideal served at tea time, though any or all of the desserts are also splendid served after dinner.

The sorbets can be prepared a day or two in advance; just be sure to take them out of the freezer a half hour or so before serving so they'll be scoopable. The ricotta dessert can be made several hours in advance. The fruit salads will taste and look their best if you mix them up no more than an hour before your guests arrive.

Since fruit plays a key role in the recipes, serve the desserts on white porcelain or brightly colored tableware that shows off the desserts' fresh, bright colors to greatest advantage. Decorate your table with a crisp, bright white or cool pastel cloth and vases of fresh seasonal flowers. Vivaldi or other sprightly classical music would be just right.

M E N U

Seasonal Berry Salad

Gingered Melon Salad

Tropical Sorbet Medley

Ricotta-Raisin Ramekins

Light Cookies

Coffee and Select Herbal Teas

For 8 to 10 people

Seasonal Berry Salad

This fruit salad couldn't be easier, so there's really no recipe to speak of! Just aim to have about 1/3 to 1/2 cup total of berries per guest, and make your selection from the freshest, most beautiful fruits your supermarket or produce store has to offer—strawberries (left whole if small, halved or sliced if large), raspberries, blueberries, blackberries, boysenberries and more.

Choose only those whose taste matches their physical perfection, and there'll be no need to sweeten this salad with sugar or sugar substitutes. Keep the berry varieties separate, chilling in the refrigerator, and gently toss them together in a roomy serving bowl moments before the party begins.

Gingered Melon Salad

There's a seductive, almost musky perfume to a good melon, and that quality is enhanced by a simple sprinkling of powdered ginger and a drizzle of honey. This recipe works well with firm, ripe cantaloupe or honeydew or both.

Toss this salad together no more than 15 minutes before guests arrive, or the melon's juices will be drawn out and the salad will become a touch too messy, though no less delicious.

1 chilled ripe, firm cantaloupe, halved, seeded and scooped with a melon baller

1 chilled ripe, firm honeydew, halved, seeded and scooped with a melon baller

1 teaspoon powdered ginger

2 tablespoons honey, at room temperature

1 teaspoon fresh lemon juice

1 teaspoon fresh lime juice

Put the cantaloupe and honeydew balls in a large mixing bowl. Sprinkle evenly and finely with the ginger and toss gently.

Drizzle the honey evenly over the melon and sprinkle with the lemon and lime juice. Toss gently and serve.

Makes 8 to 10 servings

© Gordon E. Smith

Tropical Sorbet Medley

Fresh tropical fruits have a vivid, heady taste that's the perfect counterpart to their vibrant neon colors. The recipe below gives instructions for 1 batch of basic sorbet. Select 2 or 3 varieties of tropical fruit—mango, papaya, pineapple, passion fruit, kiwi and so on—that are available and in best condition, and serve them together in small scoops placed attractively side by side in shallow chilled bowls.

The flavor and texture of the sorbets will be at their best the fresher they are. So mix and freeze them no more than 24 hours ahead of time, and take them out of your freezer 30 minutes or so before serving so they'll be scoopable at party time.

2/3 cup water

1/2 cup sugar

3 cups pureed and sieved tropical fruit (for passion fruit, pass the seedy pulp through a sieve, without pureeing)

Put the sugar and water in a small saucepan over medium to low heat. Simmer for 5 minutes, stirring occasionally.

Stir together the sugar-water syrup and the fruit puree and freeze in an ice-cream maker, following manufacturer's directions.

Makes 8 to 10 servings

Ricotta-Raisin Ramekins

You can make the individual ramekins several hours ahead and chill them, covered, in the refrigerator.

1/2 cup seedless golden raisins

1/2 cup Marsala wine

2 pounds skimmed-milk ricotta cheese, well drained

1 cup confectioners' sugar

1 tablespoon orange juice

1 teaspoon lemon juice

1 tablespoon grated orange zest

1/2 tablespoon grated lemon zest

2 egg whites, beaten until soft peaks form

10 thin strips each orange and lemon zest

Put the raisins and Marsala in a small bowl or measuring cup and leave to soak for about 30 minutes.

In a mixing bowl, stir together the ricotta, sugar, orange and lemon juice, and grated zests until smoothly blended. Then fold and blend in the egg whites.

Spoon the mixture into individual serving ramekins, cover and chill in the refrigerator. Garnish with strips of orange and lemon zest.

Makes 10 servings

Light Cookies

To complement the flavors of the fresh fruit desserts, serve a light, crisp cookie such as the Pecan Butter Cookies (page 135), almond tuiles (page 134) made without their Florentine chocolate dip or any favorite, light, quality cookies from your market, gourmet shop or bakery.

Autumn Pie
and
Cobbler Party

No desserts are more comforting than pies and cobblers. As the autumn days chill, or when the winter winds blow, these desserts warm and sustain us in a simple way. Imagine your guests trudging up the walkway through an afternoon's bracing winds, icy rain or swirling snow, only to enter your home and be greeted by the heady aroma of just-baked treats.

You, of course, will have done most of the preparation the night or morning before the party, making the piecrust dough and assembling the pies and cobblers. To make things easier, the three main desserts all make use of the same basic crust recipe, which you'll find with the crumble-topped apple pie.

Get the oven preheating about an hour and a half before the party begins, and put the various desserts in at the right moment so they'll be ready to serve—just minutes out of the oven—when guests arrive.

Set the table with your most rustic pottery, complemented by checked or country floral-print napery and by arrangements of dried flowers and any other country-style decorations or folk art you might have. Pick up a few albums of country fiddle music, or set a more refined but no less down-home tone with the all-American music of Aaron Copland.

Crumble-Topped Apple Pie with Walnuts and Raisins

A homey crumble topping made with crushed gingersnaps and walnuts and raisins mixed into the filling gives special distinction to this country-style deep-dish pie.

Make all the various elements of the pies the day or night before, so you're ready to start assembling and baking them about 1½ hours or so before the party starts.

Piecrust

3 cups all-purpose flour

2 tablespoons confectioners' sugar

1 teaspoon salt

3/4 cup chilled unsalted butter, cut into 1/2-inch pieces

1/4 cup chilled vegetable shortening

1/2 to 2/3 cup ice water

M E N U

Crumble-Topped Apple Pie with Walnuts and Raisins

Individual Pear and Almond Cobblers

Mandarin Orange Tartlets

Sharp Cheddar Cheese and Crackers

Assorted Nuts and Dried Fruits

Mulled Cider

Hot Coffee and Tea

For 10 to 12 people

Crumble Topping

2 1/2 cups finely crumbled gingersnaps

1 cup packed brown sugar

3/4 cup rolled oats

3/4 cup finely chopped walnuts

1 cup unsalted butter, melted

Filling

5 pounds baking apples, peeled, cored and sliced

1 1/2 cups packed brown sugar

1/2 cup honey

1/2 cup coarsely chopped walnuts

1/2 cup seedless raisins

1/3 cup cornstarch

1/2 tablespoon cinnamon

1 teaspoon grated nutmeg

1 teaspoon grated orange zest

For the crust, put the flour, sugar and salt in a processor with the metal blade and pulse 3 or 4 times to mix. Add the butter and shortening, and pulse the machine until the mixture resembles coarse gravel.

With the machine running, pour 1/2 cup of the water through the feed tube and continue processing until the dough begins to come together, adding a little extra water if necessary. Empty the contents of the bowl onto a floured work surface and gently knead the dough just until it is smooth, gathering it into a ball. Divide the dough in half, wrap in wax paper and refrigerate.

For the crumble topping, in a mixing bowl stir together the gingersnap crumbs, sugar, oats and walnuts. Add the melted butter, and stir until the mixture resembles coarse crumbs. Cover and store at cool room temperature or refrigerate.

Preheat the oven to 350°F.

Meanwhile, for the filling, in a large mixing bowl stir together the apples, sugar, honey, walnuts, raisins, cornstarch, cinnamon, nutmeg and orange zest.

On a lightly floured surface, roll out the 2 balls of piecrust into circles about 12 inches in diameter. Use the circle to line 2 nine-inch, deep-dish pie pans, trimming the crusts even with the edge of the pan. Prick the crusts all over with a fork, and bake them in the preheated oven for about 10 minutes.

Divide the filling between the 2 pie pans, and cover evenly with the crumble topping. Bake the pies, together or one at a time, until golden and bubbling, about 50 minutes.

Let the pies cool for 10 to 15 minutes before slicing and serving.

Makes two 9-inch pies

Individual Pear and Almond Cobblers

Choose firm cooking pears for this dish, to ensure that the fruit retains some texture after baking.

Prepare the pear and almond filling and the cobbler dough the night before. All you have left to do, just an hour or so before guests start arriving, is fill serving-size baking dishes with the pear mixture, top each with a piece of dough and then bake them.

If guests like, they can eat their cobblers right out of the dishes. Or they can lift off the crust, place it on a serving plate and spoon the filling on top.

Piecrust

(see recipe on page 98)

Filling

1¹/4 cups dry apple cider

1 cup packed brown sugar

1 teaspoon ground cinnamon

1/2 teaspoon grated nutmeg

14 large cooking pears, cored and cut into 1/2-inch pieces

1/4 cup cornstarch

3/4 cup slivered almonds

1/2 cup unsalted butter, softened

2 cups heavy cream

Prepare the piecrust and, without dividing it, wrap and refrigerate it.

For the filling, put the cider, sugar, cinnamon and nutmeg in a heavy saucepan, and bring to a boil over medium heat, stirring constantly to dissolve the sugar. Add the pears and continue cooking just until they are barely tender, about 5 minutes. Remove from the heat and let the pears cool in the liquid. Then drain off 1/2 cup of the liquid and sprinkle in the cornstarch, stirring to dissolve. Gently stir the cornstarch mixture and the almonds back into the pears.

Preheat the oven to 350°F.

Spoon the pear-and-almond mixture into 12 individual ovenproof cobbler dishes. Dot the filling with butter. Divide the dough into 12 equal pieces, and roll or flatten each piece to a shape that covers each cobbler dish to the rim. Place the cobbler dishes in the oven (in 2 or more batches, if necessary, depending on oven size) and bake until the crusts are golden, 45 to 50 minutes. Serve hot from the oven, lightly drizzled, if your guests like, with heavy cream.

Makes 12 individual cobblers

© Burke/Triolo

Mandarin Orange Tartlets

These simply made tartlets seem to capture all the warmth of summer sunshine in the bright taste and color of mandarin oranges.

Bake up the shells (in 2 batches, if necessary), and make the filling a day or so in advance. Store the shells in an airtight container, and keep the filling covered in the refrigerator. The morning of the party, you can fill the tartlets, top them with the mandarin segments and glaze them; keep them covered in the refrigerator until serving.

Tartlet Shells

Piecrust (see recipe on page 98)

1/4 cup unsalted butter, melted

Citrus Pastry Cream

3 cups milk

1 whole vanilla bean, split in half lengthwise

1 cup sugar

1/2 cup all-purpose flour

1/8 teaspoon salt

4 whole eggs, lightly beaten

4 egg yolks, lightly beaten

2 tablespoons grated orange zest

1 tablespoon grated lemon zest

Glaze and Filling

1 cup apricot jam

2 tablespoons orange-flavored liqueur

6 cups mandarin orange segments, drained if canned

Prepare the piecrust and, without dividing it, wrap and refrigerate it.

To make the tartlet shells, preheat the oven to 350°F. Use the dough to line 24 round 3¼-inch tartlet molds. Lightly brush the dough with melted butter and bake the shells for 35 to 40 minutes, or until golden brown. Let the shells cool, then store in an airtight container until ready to use.

For the pastry cream, first put the milk and vanilla bean in a heavy saucepan and bring to a boil over medium heat. Set aside.

In a mixing bowl, stir together the sugar, flour and salt. Add the eggs and egg yolks and, with a wire whisk, beat until thoroughly combined, thick and creamy.

Remove the vanilla bean from the hot milk. Whisking continuously, slowly pour the milk into the egg mixture. Pour the mixture through a strainer back into the saucepan, and cook over medium to low heat, stirring continuously, until it just comes to a boil.

Remove the pan from the heat, stir in the orange and lemon zests, and let the pastry cream cool, stirring occasionally to help the cooling and to prevent a skin from forming. Transfer the pastry cream to a bowl, cover it with plastic wrap and refrigerate.

For the glaze, in a small saucepan over low heat, melt the apricot jam with the liqueur, stirring to combine them. Pour the mixture through a sieve into a bowl, and let it cool while you assemble the tartlets.

Spoon or pipe the pastry cream into the baked shells, filling them about halfway. Arrange mandarin segments in a spiral or sunburst pattern on top of the filling.

Evenly brush the glaze over the tartlets. Refrigerate until serving time.

Makes 2 dozen tartlets

Sharp Cheddar Cheese, Crackers, Assorted Nuts and Dried Fruits

Offer your guests an assortment of other nibbles to complement the desserts.

Sharp Cheddar cheese contrasts nicely with the tastes of apples and pears; buy a good, 1-pound wedge and present it with an assortment of crackers.

Also set out a shallow tray piled with nuts in their shells—and a nutcracker or two, of course—and an arrangement of dried fruits such as apricots, pears, apple rings, peaches and so on.

Mulled Cider

Hot, spiced cider is the perfect, bracing drink to serve your guests on a blustery day.

Set the mixture to mulling at least a half an hour before people are slated to arrive.

1 gallon apple cider

1/2 cup raisins

4 cinnamon sticks, broken into 1-inch pieces

1 teaspoon whole cloves

Zest of 2 medium oranges, cut into thin strips

Zest of 1 medium lemon, cut into thin strips

1 cup brandy (optional)

Whole cinnamon sticks, for garnish

Put the cider, raisins, broken cinnamon sticks, cloves and orange and lemon zest into a large pot. Cook over medium heat until the mixture is hot but not yet boiling; reduce the heat to low, and let the mixture steep, covered, for at least 15 minutes.

Before serving, stir in the brandy if you like; or reserve it to lace individual servings. Ladle the hot cider into heavy mugs, garnishing each serving with a whole cinnamon stick.

© Steven Mark Needham/Envision

Ice Cream and Frozen Yogurt Sundae Bar

It's the quintessential, all-American summertime dessert event: a table brimming with freshly frozen treats and an assortment of toppings with which each guest can create his or her own unique dessert. Serve it after dinner on one of those long summer evenings or on a hot weekend afternoon.

Even though you're making the ice creams and frozen yogurts from scratch, they can be prepared at your leisure up to several days ahead of time, to be stored in the freezer until half an hour before the party starts, when you take them out to soften. Pack the ice cream in smaller—say, 1-quart to 1/2-gallon—freezer containers, and you can take it out of the freezer in batches, so you're always serving it in optimum condition. (It's also fair to cheat and buy your favorite flavors of frozen desserts.)

For serving, set the containers of ice cream and yogurt inside attractive bowls filled with crushed ice that you replenish as it melts. Make sure there's a good, sturdy scoop for each flavor of ice cream. Surround the featured performers with smaller bowls filled with the various supporting players, making sure there's a serving spoon for each. It's a good idea to have at least twice as many bowls and spoons as guests, since some people will want a fresh bowl for their second or third sundae.

M E N U

Extra-Rocky Rocky Road Ice Cream

Very Berry Ice Cream

Cappuccino Frozen Yogurt

Apricot-and-Almond Frozen Yogurt

Old-Fashioned Marshmallow Sauce

Assorted Classic Sprinkle-On Toppings

Bittersweet Chocolate Sauce

Assorted Chopped Fresh Fruits

For 24 to 30 people

Extra-Rocky Rocky Road Ice Cream

This version of the ice cream favorite is chock-full of nuts, marshmallow bits and other unexpected treats.

You can make the ice cream up to a week ahead of time.

1 quart half-and-half

1/2 pound unsweetened cooking chocolate, grated

1/2 tablespoon vanilla extract

6 egg yolks

2 eggs

1 cup sugar

1/2 cup coarsely chopped semisweet chocolate

1/2 cup coarsely chopped white chocolate

1/2 cup roasted almond halves

1/2 cup coarsely chopped walnuts

1/2 cup seedless raisins

1/2 cup miniature marshmallows

In a heavy saucepan, heat the half-and-half over medium heat until bubbles begin to form around the edge of the pan. Reduce the heat to low, and add the grated chocolate, stirring until it melts. Remove the pan from the heat, and stir in the vanilla.

In the top half of a double boiler, away from the heat, whisk the egg yolks, eggs and sugar until thick and frothy. Whisking continuously, slowly pour in about 1 cup of the half-and-half mixture. Then, over simmering water, stir in the remainder and cook the mixture, stirring continuously, until it is thick and creamy.

Pour the mixture into a glass bowl and refrigerate until cold. Then freeze in a commercial ice-cream maker, following manufacturer's directions. When the mixture is thick and frozen but still fairly soft, add the chopped chocolate, nuts, raisins and marshmallows. Then continue processing until completely frozen.

Makes about 3 quarts

Very Berry Ice Cream

Fresh berries star in this special summer-time ice cream. By all means substitute more of one kind of berry for another, depending on what's available and in peak condition.

Start making the ice cream at least the evening before. You can prepare it up to a week in advance.

5 cups heavy cream

1 cup sugar

1 whole vanilla bean

2 cups fresh strawberries

1¹/₂ cups fresh raspberries

1¹/₂ cups fresh blackberries

Put the cream, sugar and vanilla in a heavy saucepan and stir over medium heat until the sugar has dissolved and the mixture is hot but not yet boiling. Set the pan aside, covered, to cool.

Meanwhile, put all the berries in a processor with the metal blade and puree. Pour and press the puree through a fine sieve set over a mixing bowl to remove the seeds. Cover the bowl and chill the puree in the refrigerator.

Remove the vanilla bean, transfer the cream to a bowl and refrigerate until well chilled.

Pour the cream and the berry puree together into a commercial ice-cream maker, and freeze following manufacturer's directions.

Makes about 3 quarts

© Tony Generico/FPG International

Cappuccino Frozen Yogurt

This popular flavor combines the tastes of chocolate and espresso coffee.

For an extra-rich version, use whole milk yogurt; or reduce the calories even more by using nonfat yogurt instead of lowfat.

Make the yogurt several hours to a day or more in advance; it keeps well in the freezer for up to a week.

2 quarts plain lowfat yogurt

1²/₃ cups sugar

1 cup brewed espresso coffee

2/3 cup unsweetened cocoa powder

1/4 cup finely ground espresso coffee beans

1/2 tablespoon vanilla extract

Put 2 cups of the yogurt, the sugar, brewed espresso (made with an espresso machine or American style, on the strong side), cocoa powder, ground espresso and vanilla in a processor with the metal blade, and pulse until smoothly blended. In a large mixing bowl, stir this mixture together with the remaining yogurt. Cover and refrigerate for 1 to 2 hours.

Put the mixture in a commercial ice-cream maker, and freeze following manufacturer's directions.

Makes about 3 quarts

Apricot-and-Almond Frozen Yogurt

The natural affinity between the tastes of fresh apricots and almonds really comes through in this frozen treat.

If you want to make an extra-rich dessert, use whole milk yogurt. Or go even lower in calories by substituting nonfat yogurt for the lowfat.

Make the yogurt several hours to a day or more in advance; it keeps well in the freezer for up to a week.

1¹/₂ cups packed fresh, skinned and sliced apricots

1¹/₂ cups sugar

1¹/₂ quarts plain lowfat yogurt

1 teaspoon almond extract

1/2 teaspoon vanilla extract

2 cups toasted slivered almonds

In a processor or blender, puree the apricots with 1 cup of the sugar.

Put the apricots, yogurt and almond and vanilla extracts in an ice-cream maker, and start to freeze them, following manufacturer's instructions.

When the yogurt mixture is thick and frozen but still fairly soft, add the almonds. Then continue processing until completely frozen.

Makes about 3 quarts

© Fredric Stein/FPG International

Old-Fashioned Marshmallow Sauce

Marshmallows are one of those mysterious confections that just seem to spring from nature preformed. Actually, they're a combination of beaten egg whites, sugar, syrup and gelatin. They melt beautifully to make this voluptuous, old-fashioned ice cream topping.

Make the marshmallow sauce several hours to a day in advance, storing it covered in the refrigerator. Serve it chilled or at room temperature.

4 egg whites

2 cups sugar

1/4 cup light corn syrup

1/2 cup milk

1/2 cup water

1¹/2 pounds white marshmallows, cut into 1/4- to 1/2-inch pieces

2 teaspoons vanilla extract

In a large mixing bowl, beat the egg whites with an electric beater until they form stiff peaks. Set them aside.

In a large, heavy saucepan over medium to low heat, stir together the sugar, syrup, milk and water until the sugar dissolves. Bring to a boil, then reduce the heat and simmer gently for about 5 minutes.

Remove the pan from the heat and gently stir in the marshmallows, just until they begin to melt. Set the pan aside for a few minutes.

Beating continuously with an electric beater, gradually pour the hot marshmallow mixture into the beaten egg whites to make a smooth, thick sauce. Add the vanilla and continue beating until the sauce cools to room temperature.

Serve the sauce chilled or at room temperature in a bowl with a large serving spoon.

Makes about 6 cups

Assorted Classic Sprinkle-On Toppings

Set out bowls of your favorite dry ice cream toppings, each with their own small serving spoon to encourage your guests to help themselves without taking *too* much.

For 2 dozen or more people, have at least 6 cups total of at least 4 different dry toppings. Choose from whole, chopped or slivered nuts, separate or mixed; bittersweet, milk or white chocolate chips or chunks or shavings; chocolate sprinkles (also known as Jimmies); multicolored sprinkles; chopped or broken pieces of candy bar; jelly beans; coarsely crumbled Oreos or other favorite cookies; raisins, plain or coated with chocolate or yogurt; chopped dried fruits; shredded coconut; and any other sweet things that strike your fancy.

Bittersweet Chocolate Sauce

Sometimes the simplest things are the best. This sauce is incredibly easy to make and tastes wonderful.

Prepare the sauce an hour or two before the party starts and keep it covered in the refrigerator. Let it sit at room temperature for at least 15 minutes before the party starts. Serve from a cup with a good, drip-free pouring spout, or from a bowl with a small sauce ladle or large serving spoon.

3/4 pound unsweetened cooking chocolate, coarsely chopped

3 cups sugar

1¹/2 cups milk

1¹/2 cups water

1/2 teaspoon salt

1 tablespoon vanilla extract

Put the chocolate, sugar, milk, water and salt in the top of a double boiler, and stir over low heat until the chocolate melts, the sugar dissolves and the sauce is smooth. Stir in the vanilla.

Transfer to a bowl and let cool to room temperature before serving.

Makes about 6 cups

Assorted Chopped Fresh Fruits

Fresh fruits do appear on some soda fountain sundaes, but they became really popular with the advent of frozen yogurt shops.

For 2 dozen or more people, have at least 6 cups total of whole, sliced or chopped fresh fruit. Among the appealing choices are bananas, all kinds of berries, pitted cherries, kiwis, mangoes, nectarines, peaches and pineapple.

Chocoholic Heaven

*S*it down and make a roster of confirmed chocoholics you count as friends. There are probably quite a number of them. And there you have it: the guest list for one of the most outrageous dessert parties you could ever dream of hosting.

Warn those guests of what's to come—a lineup of intense chocolate tastes that may make them want to go easy on whatever they eat for dinner before the party. If you want to give them a little more time to recover from this feast, you might want to throw it on a weekend afternoon.

A number of the recipes, including the truffles, the shortbreads and the sorbet, can be prepared several days in advance. You can make the cake up to a day ahead and, as long as you store it in an airtight container, still be certain that it's at its most moist and dense when you serve it.

This party works as either a casual event, with simple platters and plates and your guests in baggy clothes that keep them comfortable as they eat their way across the table, or as a drop-dead-glamorous party, with the desserts presented on your best silver and china and your guests turned out in fine clothes worthy of the sublime sweets they're about to taste. Cool jazz or Mozart works as background music for the latter party; rock or jazz would set the right tone for the casual event.

M E N U

Double Chocolate Irish Cream Fudge Cake

Individual Mexican Chocolate Mousses

Mandarin Chocolate Sherbet

Scotch Chocolate Shortbreads

Chocolate White-Chocolate-Chip Cookies

Chocolate Truffle Tasting

Dark-Roast Coffee or Espresso and Chocolate Liqueur Tasting

For 12 to 18 people

Double Chocolate Irish Cream Fudge Cake

This classic layer cake offers a double dose of intense chocolate flavor—in the cake itself and in its rich, fudgy filling and frosting—and gains an extra hint of moist, rich flavor from the addition of Irish cream-style liqueur.

Make the cake at least a day ahead. Kept airtight in a cool place, the cake will stay moist and flavorful for 2 to 3 days.

Irish Cream Fudge Cake

1 1/4 cups sugar

1/2 cup unsalted butter, at room temperature

2 eggs

2 cups all-purpose flour

6 tablespoons unsweetened cocoa powder

1 teaspoon salt

1 teaspoon baking soda

3/4 cup milk

1/4 cup Irish cream-style liqueur

1 teaspoon vanilla extract

Fudge Frosting

1/4 pound unsweetened baking chocolate, coarsely chopped

1/4 cup unsalted butter

1/4 cup warm water

1 tablespoon vanilla extract

1/8 teaspoon salt

3 cups sifted confectioners' sugar

For the cake, preheat the oven to 350°F. Grease two round 8-inch layer cake pans.

In a mixing bowl, use an electric beater to cream together the sugar and butter until smooth and light in color. One at a time, beat in the eggs until thoroughly incorporated.

In a separate bowl, stir together the flour, cocoa, salt and baking soda until thoroughly blended; in yet another bowl, combine the milk, Irish cream and vanilla.

Add about a quarter of the flour mixture to the butter mixture, beating until well blended; then beat in about a quarter of the milk mixture. Continue alternately adding the dry and wet ingredients until

thoroughly combined to form a smooth batter.

Divide the batter evenly between the 2 prepared pans, and bake until a toothpick inserted into the center comes out clean, about 35 minutes. Cool the pans on wire racks for 5 to 10 minutes; then unmold onto the racks and cool to room temperature.

While the cakes are cooling, prepare the frosting. In a double boiler over low heat, melt the chocolate and butter together. Stir in the water, vanilla and salt.

Away from the heat, gradually sprinkle and whisk in the confectioners' sugar to make a smooth frosting.

Place 1 cake layer on top of a cake platter or cardboard cake platform. Spread some of the frosting on top of the layer, and place the other layer on top. Then, with a narrow spatula, spread the remaining frosting all over the top and side of the layer cake.

Store in an airtight container until serving. Cut into thin wedges.

Makes 1 eight-inch cake

© Steven Mark Needham/Envision

Individual Mexican Chocolate Mousses

Nothing offsets the flavor of chocolate more distinctively and classically than the taste of strong coffee, and nothing complements those two flavors more enticingly than cinnamon. The three distinctive ingredients are combined here in a rich, creamy mousse served in individual dishes.

 Prepare the mousse mixture up to 24 hours in advance, and remove it from the freezer at least 30 minutes before serving. Serve it in wine glasses or small glass bowls that you have chilled in the freezer for at least 30 minutes.

1 cup heavy cream

3/4 pound semisweet chocolate, broken into 1-inch pieces

1 teaspoon ground cinnamon

1/2 cup hot espresso-strength brewed coffee

6 egg yolks

12 egg whites, at room temperature

1/4 cup confectioners' sugar

1 teaspoon vanilla extract

1/2 teaspoon coffee extract

18 (2-inch) cinnamon sticks

In a heavy saucepan, heat the heavy cream over medium heat until bubbles just begin to form around the edges.

Put the chocolate and cinnamon in a processor with the metal blade, and pulse until coarsely chopped. With the machine running, pour in the hot cream and espresso. Continue processing until the chocolate has melted and the mixture is smooth and thick, 30 to 45 seconds. Scrape down the bowl. With the machine running, add the egg yolks and continue processing until the mixture is smooth, about 20 seconds more. Set the mixture aside.

In a mixing bowl, beat the egg whites until they form stiff peaks. With a rubber spatula, gradually fold the chocolate mixture into the egg whites until smoothly blended.

Divide the mixture evenly among 18 individual serving containers. Cover them and refrigerate until the mousse is chilled and set, at least 3 hours.

Before serving, beat the whipping cream until it forms firm peaks, gradually adding the confectioners' sugar and vanilla and coffee extracts. Pipe or spoon a dollop of the whipped cream in the center of each serving of mousse, and garnish each by standing a piece of cinnamon stick at an angle at one side.

Makes 18 servings

Mandarin Chocolate Sherbet

Suave and icy, this classic ice joins the intense bittersweet flavor of chocolate with the sharp tang of mandarin oranges or tangerines.

To enjoy the sherbet at its best, mix it up and freeze it no more than 24 hours in advance. Be sure to take it out of your freezer some 30 minutes before serving so it will soften sufficiently for scooping. Serve in wine glasses or small glass bowls, prechilled in the freezer for at least 30 minutes.

2 cups unsweetened cocoa powder

1 1/4 cups sugar

1/8 teaspoon salt

1 1/2 cups lowfat milk

2 1/2 cups strained fresh mandarin or tangerine juice

1/4 cup grated mandarin or tangerine zest

3 egg whites, at room temperature

In a heavy saucepan away from the heat, stir together the cocoa powder, sugar and salt. With a wooden spoon, slowly stir in the milk, taking care to smooth out any lumps; then stir in the orange juice.

Bring the mixture to a boil over medium heat, stirring constantly to dissolve the cocoa and sugar completely. Reduce the heat and simmer, stirring continuously, for about 5 minutes. Remove the pan from the heat.

Pour the mixture into a glass bowl set inside a large bowl of ice, and stir until it has cooled completely. Add the grated zest. Then begin freezing in a commercial ice-cream maker, following manufacturer's directions.

Meanwhile, beat the egg whites until soft peaks form. When the sherbet mixture is thick but still fairly slushy, add the egg whites to the freezer and continue processing until completely frozen.

Makes about 1 1/2 quarts

Scotch Chocolate Shortbreads

Scotland's great gift to the cookie world is further enhanced here with the addition of cocoa powder. If you want to make them even more wicked, you might consider dipping them in melted chocolate.

Bake the shortbreads up to 3 days ahead, storing them in an airtight container to maintain their crispness.

1 pound unsalted butter, at room temperature

1²/₃ cups confectioners' sugar

2²/₃ cups all-purpose flour

2 cups self-raising flour

2/3 cup unsweetened cocoa powder

1/4 teaspoon salt

Preheat the oven to 350°F.

In a mixing bowl, cream together the butter and sugar until smooth, light and fluffy.

In a separate bowl, sift together the flours, cocoa powder and salt. With a pastry blender, gradually work the flour mixture into the creamed mixture, adding just enough to make a firm but soft dough. Gently and briefly, knead the dough on a floured work surface just until smooth.

Divide the dough into 2 equal portions. Gently and evenly press each into an ungreased 8-inch-square baking pan. With a fork, prick the surface of the dough all over.

Bake the shortbread just until very lightly browned, no more than about an hour. Remove the pan from the oven and, with the tip of a table knife, score the shortbread—cutting no more than about a quarter of the way through—into 16 equal 1-by-4-inch fingers per pan.

Let the shortbread cool and harden. Then unmold and break by hand into individual pieces. Store in an airtight container.

Makes 32 shortbreads

© Burke/Triolo

Chocolate White-Chocolate-Chip Cookies

Imagine looking at a black-and-white negative of a photograph of classic Tollhouse™ cookies, and you'll get a pretty good idea of the startling visual effect of these cookies—a dark chocolate dough combined with white chocolate chips.

You can bake the cookies up to 3 days ahead, storing them in an airtight container.

1 cup unsalted butter

1¹/₂ cups granulated sugar

1/2 cup packed brown sugar

2 eggs

2 teaspoons vanilla extract

1 teaspoon almond extract

2 cups all-purpose flour

6 tablespoons unsweetened cocoa powder

1 teaspoon salt

1 teaspoon baking soda

2¹/₂ cups white chocolate chips

Preheat the oven to 375°F.

In a mixing bowl, cream together the butter, granulated and brown sugars, eggs and vanilla and almond extracts until light and fluffy.

In a separate bowl, sift together the flour, cocoa, salt and baking soda. Add them to the creamed mixture and blend thoroughly. Then stir in the white chocolate chips.

Drop generous teaspoonfuls of the batter about 2 inches apart on greased cookie sheets, and bake until lightly browned, 10 to 12 minutes. With a spatula, transfer the cookies to a wire rack to cool. Store in an airtight container.

Makes about 6 dozen cookies

© Steven Mark Needham/Envision

Chocolate Truffle Tasting

Make up several half batches of chocolate truffles (see recipe on page 57), flavoring each half batch differently and offering a visual clue to what its flavor is. Arrange them in rows, by flavor, on an attractive serving tray. Tell your guests which flavors are which—or let them test their taste-buds and guess!

Some suggestions:

Cherry Truffles. Place a candied or brandied cherry at the center of each truffle, with its stem coming out of the top. Flavor the truffle mixture with cherry brandy.

Coffee Truffles. Flavor with Kahlua or Tia Maria, and garnish with a chocolate-covered coffee bean.

Mint Truffles. Flavor the mixture with peppermint schnapps or a mint-flavored liqueur, and top each truffle with a candied mint leaf.

Orange Truffles. Use Grand Marnier or Cointreau liqueur and a little grated orange zest in the truffle mixture, and decorate the top of each truffle with a small piece of candied orange peel.

Peanut Truffles. Melt 3 tablespoons of chunky peanut butter with the other truffle ingredients, and top each truffle with a roasted peanut.

Raspberry Truffles. Flavor the mixture with framboise liqueur and decorate with a candied rose petal.

Dark-Roast Coffee or Espresso and Chocolate Liqueur Tasting

To provide strong contrast to the many chocolate tastes, brew up regular and decaffeinated pots of a strong, dark-roast coffee blend; if you have an espresso pot or machine, offer espresso. You might want to suggest to your guests that they try their coffee black and unsweetened; though you should certainly offer milk or cream and sugar to those who want it.

As an added treat, comb your local liquor store for a few bottles of the many brands of chocolate-flavored liqueur that are available. Among the possibilities: Cacao mit Nuss (German chocolate-hazelnut); Cheri Suisse (Swiss chocolate-cherry); Vandermint (Dutch chocolate-mint); Sabra (Israeli chocolate-orange); and the Royal family from France, which includes Royal Mint-Chocolate (the first of the line), Apricot-Chocolate, Banana-Chocolate, Cherry-Chocolate, Coconut-Chocolate, French Coffee-Chocolate, Fruit and Nut-Chocolate, Ginger-Chocolate, Lemon-Chocolate, Nut-Chocolate, Orange-Chocolate and Raspberry-Chocolate.

Courtesy of Williams-Sonoma

Coffee and…

*S*ometimes the perfect dessert is just a little something—that small, sweet, barely substantial taste represented by the ellipsis in the familiar phrase "coffee and...."

You know the context. Someone calls you and invites you to come over late in the morning or afternoon, or just after dinner. "We'll just have a little coffee and...." Usually, the "and..." consists of a store-bought coffee cake and some premium cookies hurriedly purchased a few hours ahead.

And there's nothing wrong with that. But with very little extra effort, you can turn this simple collection of sweet tastes into something special by making and baking your own accompaniments for coffee. The work can be done well in advance, the cookies and other little treats stored to preserve their freshness right until serving time. While the quantities here are enough for a small, casual gathering, they're easily doubled or tripled.

You don't even have to go all-out setting the table—this is, after all, an off-the-cuff event. Just put out your best everyday dishes, cups and saucers. Toss a few simple flowers—picked from your own garden or window box, perhaps—into a vase. Turn on your favorite radio station, or pop on your favorite instrumental record. And sit back to play the host or hostess, making it all look like an absolute cinch.

M E N U

Almond Tuiles

Pecan Butter Cookies

Lemon Curd Tartlets

Chocolate-Dipped Fruits and Nuts

Bowl of Fresh Fruit

Coffee (and Assorted Teas)

For 4 to 6 people

Almond Tuiles

Tuile is French for *tile*—the kind of long, curved tiles you see overlapping on the roofs of country houses and Paris apartment buildings. These crisp, ultrathin almond cookies are so-named because they mimic that roofing tile shape, having been curled over a rolling pin straight from the oven.

The cookies will keep crisp in an airtight container somewhere cool, so you can make them a few days ahead of time.

1/2 cup sugar

1/4 cup unsalted butter, cut into 1/2-inch pieces

2 tablespoons whipping cream

1 tablespoon grated orange zest

1 tablespoon grated lemon zest

3 egg whites

1/3 cup flour

Pinch of salt

1 cup slivered almonds

2 teaspoons anise seeds

Put the sugar, butter, cream and orange and lemon zests in a processor with the metal blade and process until creamed. With the machine running, add the egg whites, flour and salt. Pour the batter into a bowl, and stir in the almonds and anise seeds. Cover and refrigerate for 1 hour.

Preheat the oven to 350°F.

Butter and lightly flour a cookie sheet. Drop the batter in heaping teaspoons on the sheet, placing them at least 6 inches apart to allow room for the cookies to spread.

Bake until golden brown at the edges and pale golden in the center, about 10 minutes. As soon as you remove the tuiles from the oven, lift them carefully with a spatula, and drape them over a rolling pin to curve; after about 1 minute, when they've hardened into shape, remove to a wire rack to cool. Repeat with the remaining batter. Store the tuiles in an airtight container.

Makes about 3 dozen cookies

Pecan Butter Cookies

The classic Scandinavian butter cookie is prized for its utter simplicity—subtle flavor combined with crisp-yet-crumbly texture.

These cookies can be made up to several days in advance and will remain crisp if stored in an airtight container. Or you can simply make the dough well ahead of time, and keep it wrapped in the refrigerator, ready to slice and bake up fresh before guests arrive.

1/2 pound unsalted butter, at room temperature

1/3 cup granulated sugar

1/3 cup packed brown sugar

1 egg

1/2 teaspoon vanilla extract

2 cups all-purpose flour

1/2 cup coarsely chopped pecans

1/2 teaspoon salt

In a mixing bowl or a processor fitted with the metal blade, cream together the butter, sugars, egg and vanilla.

In a separate bowl, stir together the flour, pecans and salt. Gradually blend the dry ingredients into the creamed mixture to form a soft, firm and smooth dough.

Form the dough into a cylindrical log 12 inches long, and wrap it in wax paper. Chill in the refrigerator for at least 2 hours.

Preheat the oven to 375°F.

Unwrap the log of dough and, with a small, sharp knife, slice it into 1/4-inch-thick rounds, placing them about 1 inch apart on ungreased cookie sheets. Bake until light golden, 10 to 12 minutes; then transfer the cookies with a spatula to a wire rack to cool. Store in an airtight container.

Makes about 4 dozen cookies

Courtesy of Williams-Sonoma

Lemon Curd Tartlets

Lemon curd, a rich, tart custard made from fresh lemons and eggs, is one of the great tart fillings; here, it's made even more delightful through a combination of the juices and zests of lime and orange along with the lemon. So intense and tangy is it that it makes a perfect filling for small, individual tartlet shells. While two or three bites are perfectly satisfying, your guests will more likely than not feel compelled to have another, and maybe another.

You can prepare the lemon curd up to several days ahead and store it in a covered jar in the refrigerator; any extra you may have is excellent as a spread for breakfast or tea breads. The tartlet shells can also be baked ahead and kept in an airtight container to maintain their crispness. Shortly before guests arrive, spoon or pipe the lemon curd into the pastry shells and garnish them.

Tartlet shells

Piecrust (see recipe on page 98)

1/4 cup unsalted butter, melted

Lemon Curd

1 1/4 cups sugar

4 tablespoons unsalted butter

2 tablespoons lemon juice

2 tablespoons lime juice

1 1/2 tablespoons orange juice

Pinch of salt

3 eggs, beaten until frothy

1 teaspoon grated lemon zest

1 teaspoon grated lime zest

1 teaspoon grated orange zest

Candied violets or thin strips of lemon, lime and orange zest, for garnish

Prepare the piecrust and, without dividing it, wrap and refrigerate it.

To make the tartlet shells, preheat the oven to 350°F. Use the dough to line 24 round 3 1/4-inch tartlet molds. Lightly brush the dough with melted butter and bake the shells for 35 to 40 minutes, or until golden brown. Let the shells cool, then store in an airtight container until ready to use.

For the citrus curd, put the sugar, butter, lemon, lime and orange juices, eggs and salt in a heavy saucepan. Cook over very low heat, stirring continuously, until they form a thick, smooth custard, about 15 minutes. Stir in the grated zest, let the curd cool to room temperature, then cover and refrigerate.

Before serving, spoon or pipe the curd into the tart shells. Garnish with candied violets or citrus zest strips.

Makes 24 tartlets

© Steven Mark Needham/Envision

Chocolate-Dipped Fruits and Nuts and a Bowl of Fresh Fruits

To round out your menu, set out an attractive selection of little sweet nibbles. Make up a double batch of dipped fruits and nuts (recipe on page 59), and arrange them on a pretty tray. For guests who might be watching what they eat, be sure to also offer a bowl of fresh seasonal fruits without chocolate—including, say, grapes, berries, cherries, a few small bananas, a couple of small apples, melon, ripe peaches, strawberries, plums and nectarines.

Mail-Order Sources

The following companies supply special ingredients that may be used to prepare the recipes and menus in this book. Write for their price lists and catalogs.

Ace Pecan Co.
281 West 83rd St.
Burr Ridge, IL 60521
(708) 789-8511
pecans

American Spoon Foods
411 East Lake St.
P.O. Box 566
Petoskey, MI 49770
(616) 347-9030
fruit preserves

Balducci's Mail-order
42-25 12th St.
Long Island City, NY 11101
(800) 225-3822
gourmet specialty foods

Brumwell Flour Mill
616 Sixth Ave. West
Cresko, IA 52136
(319) 578-8106
stone-ground flours and grains

Butte Creek Mill
P.O. Box 561
Eagle Point, OR 97524
(503) 826-3531
stone-ground flours and grains

Cascade Conserves
P.O. Box 8306
Portland, OR 97207
(503) 243-3608
fruit preserves

Clearbrook Farms
5514 Fair Lane
Fairfax, OH 45227
(513) 271-2053
fruit preserves and dessert sauces

Country Estate Pecans
L & C Gourmet Products, Inc.
P.O. Box 7
Sahuarita, AZ 85629
(602) 791-2062
pecans

Dean & Deluca
560 Broadway
New York, NY 10012
(212) 431-1691
(800) 221-7714
gourmet specialty foods

Dearborn
1 Christopher St.
New York, NY 10014
(212) 691-9153
dessert sauces and chocolate truffle kits

Dundee Orchards
P.O. Box 327
Dundee, OR 97115
(503) 538-8105
hazelnuts

Gillies Coffee Company
150 19th St.
Brooklyn, NY 11232
(718) 499-7766
gourmet coffees

Gourmet Nut Center
P.O. Box 845
Orlando, CA 95963
(916) 865-5511
gourmet nuts

Grace Tea Company Limited
50 West 17th St.
New York, NY 10011
(212) 255-2935
gourmet teas

Grace's Market Place
1237 Third Ave.
New York, NY 10021
(212) 737-0600
gourmet specialty foods

Grand Finale
200 Hillcrest Rd.
Berkeley, CA 94705
(510) 655-8414
dessert sauces and buttercream caramels

Susan Green's California Cuisine
3501 Taylor Dr.
Ukiah, CA 94582
(800) 753-8558

Harney & Sons Limited Fine Teas
P.O. Box 676
Salisbury, CT 06068
(203) 435-9218
gourmet teas

Harry and David
Bear Creek Orchards
Medford, OR 97501
(503) 776-2400
fresh fruits and other gourmet items

Hawaiian Plantations
650 Iwilei Road
Honolulu, HI 96817
(808) 545-4554
pineapples, preserves, macadamias

Mariani Nut Company
P.O. Box 808
Winters, CA 95694
(916) 795-3311
gourmet nuts and dried fruits

Moon Shine Trading Company
P.O. Box 896
Winters, CA 95964
(916) 795-3207
gourmet honeys

Nunes Farms Almonds
P.O. Box 146
San Anselmo, CA 94960
(415) 459-7201
almonds

Oregon Apiaries
P.O. Box 1078
Newberg, OR 97132
(503) 538-8546
gourmet honeys

Paradigm Chocolate Co.
5775 SW Jean Road
Suite 106A
Lake Oswego, OR 97035
(503) 636-4880
dessert sauces

The Peanut Patch
P.O. Box 186
Courtland, VA 23837
(804) 653-2028
peanuts

Rocky Top Farms
Route 1, Essex Rd.
Ellsworth, MI 49729
(616) 599-2251
fruit preserves and toppings

Sable & Rosenfeld
89 McCaul St.
Suite 225
Toronto, ONT M5T 2X7
Canada
(416) 929-4214
preserves, jams, and other gourmet items

Linda Sahagian & Associates, Inc.
124 Madison St.
Oak Park, IL 60302
(708) 848-5552
Belgian chocolate, fondue pots

St. Moritz Chocolatier
510 Madison Ave.
New York, NY 10022
(212) 486-0265
chocolates and chocolate sauces

Sarabeth's Kitchen
423 Amsterdam Ave.
New York, NY 10024
(212) 496-6280
fruit preserves

The Silver Palate
274 Columbus Ave.
New York, NY 10023
(212) 799-6340
dessert sauces and fruit preserves

Starbucks Coffee and Tea Mail Order
P.O. Box 34510
2203 Airport Way South
Seattle, WA 98124-1510
(800) 445-3428
gourmet coffees and teas

Timber Crest Farms
4791 Dry Creek Rd.
Healdsburg, CA 95448
(707) 433-8251
dried fruits and nuts

Upper Canada Coffee Works & Tea Mill
612 Gordon Baker Road
Willowdale, ONT M2H 256
Canada
(416) 494-9700
coffees and teas

Additional Photo Credits